1984

KIERKEGAARD

Resources and Results

Edited and with an Introduction by

Alastair McKinnon

Recently, a conference of scholars considered resources and results in Kierkegaard research. In part one, "Resources," J. C. McLelland gives a short account of the acquisition of the Malantschuk collection by McGill University, H. P. Rohde discusses the collection as a basis for research, and H. Möller comments on its accessibility to scholars. N. J. Cappelørn examines the importance of the *Papirer* as a resource.

In part two, "Results," H. V. Hong analyzes Kierkegaard's concept of "Thought-Experiment," relating it to Kierkegaard translation. J. Walker elucidates four of Kierkegaard's assumptions concerning communication and notes the difficulties these pose for creating real human community. M. Carignan's paper presents the concept of the "eternal" as a synthesizing force acting upon body, soul, and spirit. H. A. Nielsen distinguishes between two levels of indirect communication in Mark 6:45-52 and calls attention to the significance of this distinction for understanding Kierkegaard. The last two essays present the results of computer research at McGill: A. H. Khan explores the concept of passion in *Concluding Unscientific Postscript*, and A. McKinnon offers a spatial representation of the relations among Kierkegaard's thirty-four works.

The volume, containing responses by R. L. Perkins, R. Archer, P. Carpenter, D. Lochhead, D. Goicoechea, and R. Johnson, will be of interest to Kierkegaard, philosophy, and religion scholars, and those engaged in computer research in the humanities.

Alastair McKinnon is MacDonald Professor of Moral Philosophy, Chairman of the Department of Philosophy at McGill University, and a member of the Kierkegaard Academy in Copenhagen. He is the author of Falsification and Belief, The Kierkegaard Indices, *and many articles in learned journals.*

KIERKEGAARD

Resources and Results

Edited and with an Introduction by

Alastair McKinnon

Wilfrid Laurier University Press

Canadian Cataloguing in Publication Data

Main entry under title:

Kierkegaard : resources and results

Papers presented at the Kierkegaard: Resources and
Results Conference, held at McGill University,
June 6-8, 1980.
ISBN 0-919401-02-3

1. Kierkegaard, Søren, 1813-1855—Congresses.
2. Kierkegaard-Malantschuk Collection—Congresses.
3. Kierkegaard, Søren, 1813-1855—Library resources—
Congresses. I. McKinnon, Alastair, 1925-
II. Kierkegaard: Resources and Results Conference (1980 :
McGill University)

B4377.K53 198′.9 C81-090064-5

This book has been set with a NDK ROMAN PS wheel
on a Xerox Diablo 1750 terminal by
Inter Editions, 3005 Barat Road,
Montreal, Canada H3Y 2H4

Table of Contents

List of Abbreviations

The following title codes have been used in some chapters and notes in this volume.

LP	[From the Papers of one Still Living]	Af en endnu Levendes Papirer
BI	The Concept of Irony (New York, 1965)	Om Begrebet Ironi
EE1	Either/Or 1 (Princeton, 1971)	Enten-Eller. Første halvbind
EE2	Either/Or 2 (Princeton, 1971)	Enten-Eller. Andet halvbind
FB	Fear and Trembling (New York, 1954 and Princeton, 1968)	Frygt og Bæven
G	Repetition (London, 1946)	Gjentagelsen
T	Edifying Discourses 1-2 (Minneapolis, 1962)	Atten opbyggelige Taler
F	[Prefaces]	Forord
PS	Philosophical Fragments (Princeton, 1964)	Philosophiske Smuler
BA	The Concept of Dread (London, 1946 and Princeton, 1946)	Begrebet Angest
TTL	Thoughts on Crucial Situations in Human Life (Minneapolis, 1941)	Tre Taler ved tænkte Leiligheder
SV	Stages on Life's Way (Princeton, 1940 and New York, 1967)	Stadier paa Livets Vei
AE	Concluding Unscientific Postscript (London, 1945 and Princeton, 1968)	Afsluttende uvidenskabelig Efterskrift
LA	Two Ages (Princeton, 1978)	En literair Anmeldelse
OTA	Purity of Heart (New York, 1956) & The Gospel of Suffering (Minneapolis, 1948)	Opbyggelige Taler i forskjellig Aand

KG	Works of Love (New York, 1964)	Kjerlighedens Gjerninger
CT	Christian Discourses (London, 1952 and New York, 1961)	Christelige Taler
KK	Crisis in the Life of an Actress (New York, 1967)	Krisen og en Krise i en Skuespillerendes Liv
SFV	"The Point of View for my Work as an Author" in The Point of View (New York, 1962)	Synspunktet for min Forfatter Virksomhed
LF	"The Lilies of the Field and the Birds of the Air" (in CT, above)	Lilien paa Marken og Fuglen under Himlen
TSA	"Two Minor Ethico-Religious Treatises" in The Present Age (London, 1949 and New York, 1962)	Tvende ethisk-religieuse Smaa-Afhandlinger
SD	The Sickness unto Death (New York, 1954 and Princeton, 1968)	Sygdommen til Døden
YTS	"'The High Priest' - 'The Publican' - 'The Woman that was a Sinner'" (in CT, above)	"Ypperstepræsten" - "Tolderen" - "Synderinden"
IC	Training in Christianity (London, 1946 and Princeton, 1967)	Indøvelse i Christendom
EOT	"An Edifying Discourse" (in IC, above)	En opbyggelig Tale
GU	"The Unchangeableness of God" (in TS, below)	Guds Uforanderlighed
TAF	"Two Discourses at the Communion on Fridays (in TS, below)	To Taler ved Altergangen om Fredagen
FV	"On My Work as an Author" (in SFV, above)	Om min Forfatter-Virksomhed
TS	"For Self-Examination" in For Self-Examination and Judge for Yourselves! (Princeton, 1944)	Til Selvprøvelse, Samtiden anbefalet
DS	"Judge for Yourselves!" (in TS, above)	Dømmer selv!
B21	"Articles in the 'Fatherland'" (in Ø, below)	Bladartikler 1854-55 (I-XXI)
Ø	"The Instant", Nos. I-X, in Attack upon "Christendom" 1854-55 (London, 1946)	Øieblikket

HCD	"What Christ's Judgement is about Official Christianity" (in Ø, above)	Hvad Christus dømmer om officiel Christendom
BFF	A small part available as "A Passing Comment on a Detail in Don Juan", (in KK, above)	Bladartikler, der staar i Forhold til "Forfatter-skabet"

SV (I-XIV) Søren Kierkegaards samlede Værker, udg. af A. B. Drachmann, J. L. Heiberg og H. O. Lange. 1. Udg. I-XIV. Kbh. 1901-06.

SV (1-19) Søren Kierkegaards samlede Værker, udg. af A. B. Drachmann, J. L. Heiberg, H. O. Lange og Peter P. Rohde. 3. Udg. 1-20. Kbh. 1962-64.

Pap. Søren Kierkegaards Papirer, udg. af P. A. Heiberg, V. Kuhr, og E. Torsting. Anden forøgede Udg. ved Niels Thulstrup. I-XIII. Kbhvn. 1968-70. Index A-Ø og Bibelindex ved N. J. Cappelørn. XIV-XVI. Kbhvn. 1975-78.

JP (1-6) Søren Kierkegaard's Journals and Papers, trans. Howard V. Hong and Edna H. Hong. 1-7. Bloomington and London. 1967-78.

ASKB Auktionsprotokol over Søren Kierkegaards Bogsamling, udg. af H. P. Rohde. Kbhvn. 1967.

Note that simple or plain title codes or abbreviations are used to refer to individual volumes and underlined ones to a set or collection of works.

Note too that a roman number following SV indicates a volume in the first Danish edition of Kierkegaard's collected works and that an arabic number indicates a volume in the third edition of these works.

List of Tables and Figures

Cappelørn

Khan

McKinnon

Acknowledgements

Permission to quote has been kindly granted by the following:

Søren Kierkegaard, Either/Or, trans. by David F. Swenson and Lillian Marvin Swenson, by permission of Princeton University press.

Søren Kierkegaard, The Concept of Dread, trans. by Walter Lowrie, by permission of Princeton University Press.

Søren Kierkegaard, Concluding Unscientific Postscript, trans. by David F. Swenson and Walter Lowrie, by permission of Princeton University Press.

Søren Kierkegaard, Works of Love, trans. by Howard and Edna Hong, by permission of Harper & Row, Publishers, Inc.

Søren Kierkegaard, Christian Discourses, trans. by Walter Lowrie, by permission of Oxford University Press.

Søren Kierkegaard, The Point of View, trans. by Walter Lowrie, by permission of Oxford University Press.

Søren Kierkegaard, The Sickness Unto Death, trans. by Walter Lowrie, by permission of Princeton University Press.

Søren Kierkegaard, On Authority and Revelation, trans. by Walter Lowrie, by permission of Princeton University Press.

Soren Kierkegaard's Journals and Papers, trans. by Howard V. Hong and Edna H. Hong, by permission of Indiana University Press.

Walter Lowrie, Kierkegaard, by permission of Princeton University Press.

Ludwig Wittgenstein, Philosophical Investigations, trans. by G. E. M. Anscombe, by permission of Basil Blackwell.

G. Bornkamm, Jesus of Nazareth, trans. by I. and F. McLuskey, by permission of Harper & Row, Publishers, Inc.

R. H. Fuller, Interpreting the Miracles, by permission of S.C.M. Press.

B. Vawter, This Man Jesus: An Essay Toward a New Testament Christology, by permission of Doubleday and Company.

INTRODUCTION

This volume contains the invited papers and comments presented at the Kierkegaard: Resources and Results Conference held at McGill University, June 6-8, 1980, and has been assembled in response to many requests to make this part of those deliberations available to a wider public. Though there had been no thought of publishing this material, the conference was very carefully planned around the theme of Kierkegaard research and it has therefore been possible simply to follow the original programme. Many of those present remarked upon the clear focus and direction of the conference; I very much hope that these features survive in the present work.

Given the title of this volume, one might suppose that "resources" refers to the first four chapters and "results" to the last six. It is true that we originally intended the first of these words to point to the Kierkegaard-Malantschuk Collection but it shortly became obvious that it also applied to the Papirer, the Danish text of the Samlede Værker and the machine-readable version of this text together with the many computer programs which have been developed in recent years at McGill University for its processing and interpretation. At the same time it also became clear that many of the papers which at first glance appear mainly concerned with results also provide resources for further research. In short, these rather catchy terms in our title are perhaps best seen simply as but two ends of the research spectrum.

J. C. McLelland's comments deal with the history of Kierkegaard research at McGill and touch upon the circumstances surrounding the university's recent and very fortunate acquisition of the Kierkegaard-Malantschuk Collection. H. P. Rohde discusses this collection as a basis for research and, in passing, makes quite clear the importance of knowing not only what Kierkegaard wrote but, equally, what he actually read. Hans Möller's remarks reflect the library's pride in this collection and comment upon its availability to Kierkegaard scholars. N. J. Cappelørn provides both a very suggestive interpretation of Kierkegaard's thought and a convincing demonstration of the great importance of the Papirer as a research resource, the latter being perhaps particularly appropriate since the significance of these papers has not always been fully apppreciated by North American scholars. Howard Hong discusses some of the problems of translation and, in the process, sheds much light on the expression usually translated as Thought-Experiment. Jeremy Walker articulates four of Kierkegaard's assumptions concerning communication and calls attention to the difficulties which these assumptions appear to pose for the creation of any really human community. Maurice Carignan discusses the eternal as a synthesizing "third factor" in Kierkegaard's works and suggests ways in which this conception may lead to a deeper understanding of his thought. H. A. Nielsen distinguishes two levels of indirect communication and touches upon the significance of this distinction for our understanding of Kierkegaard. A. H. Khan explores the concept of passion in the Concluding Unscientific Postscript and brings out something more of its complex geography. Finally, Alastair McKinnon provides a spatial representation of the overall relation between the 34 books in the authorship, thus producing a result which, if correct, is clearly a resource for much further research. In fact, most of the papers in this collection deal with both resources and results. So much, then, for any very sharp distinction between these two equally important aspects of scholarly research.

Robert L. Perkins, Raymond Archer, Peter Carpenter, David Lochhead, David Goicoechea, and Ralph Johnson provided stimulating and suggestive comments upon the last six papers of the conference. I wish to take this opportunity to express special thanks to these participants for agreeing to condense their remarks for publication in this volume.

It should be noted that Maurice Carignan's paper was written and delivered in French and is presented here in English largely in deference to my own view that it be published in both languages so as to become available to the widest possible audience.

I take this opportunity to report that between the writing and delivery of my own paper I discovered that I had made a mistake in the last part (the dimensional analysis of my model) and that I have taken the liberty of attempting to repair this error in the final pages of the present version. There are, after all, perhaps some advantages in being the editor!

As the reader may know, this is the second Canadian Kierkegaard conference, the first having been held at the University of Windsor in June, 1976. Both conferences demonstrated the quality and depth of Canadian Kierkegaard scholarship and, together with some of our other accomplishments, help to explain its surprisingly high international reputation and esteem. The late Dr. Gregor Malantschuk's wish that his collection should come to McGill is another and much-treasured evidence of this esteem.

As remarked earlier, the immediate occasion for this conference was the recent acquisition by McGill of the extremely valuable and important Kierkegaard-Malantschuk Collection. I should like to take this opportunity to express again my profound appreciation of and thanks for all Dr. Malantschuk's many labours and accomplishments, to thank Mrs. Grethe Kjær for all she has done to make sure that his wishes were carried out, and to thank H. P. Rohde, Hans Möller, the staff of the McLennan Library, and those of the Fleeting Opportunities Programme of the Social Sciences and Humanities Research Council of Canada for all their help in this connection.

It has been suggested that these proceedings should contain a more detailed description and perhaps even a complete listing of the thousand-odd volumes in this collection. This was a very excellent suggestion but it unfortunately came to my attention only after I had already agreed to include at least most of this information as part of a microfiche edition of some of the more valuable and inaccessible works in this collection to be called The Kierkegaard-Malantschuk Collection. The first volume of this series will consist of microfiche copies of all the first life-time editions of Kierkegaard's works and a short-title list of most of the works in this collection. This volume should be available shortly and will presumably compensate for the lack of such a list in the present one.

The conference committee consisted of Maurice Carignan, Ralph Johnson, Abrahim Khan, and myself as chairman. On behalf of this committee and of all who attended the conference I take this opportunity to thank the Faculty of Graduate Studies and Research of McGill University, the Research Communications Division of the Social Sciences and Humanities Research Council of Canada, and the Quebec Ministry of Education together with its special divisions of Direction générale de l'enseignement supérieur and Le programme de formation des chercheurs et d'action concertée for providing financial assistance to make this conference possible.

I should like to take this opportunity to express my thanks to my wife, Mrs. Mildred McKinnon, for her very valuable assistance in the preparation of the text of this volume and to Mr. Lorne Glazer for the programming involved in its correction and printing. Of course, I am solely responsible for any errors which remain.

This book has been published with the help of a grant from the Canadian Federation for the Humanities using funds provided by the Social Sciences and Humanities Research Council of Canada. I hereby record my grateful thanks to both of these agencies.

Alastair McKinnon

March 1982

1

SOME HISTORICAL BACKGROUND

J. C. McLelland

On behalf of McGill University, I bid you welcome to our campus on this signal occasion; a special word of welcome to Ambassador Korsbæk and Mrs. Korsbæk from Ottawa. This conference concerns one who has been well served by scholars such as yourselves, now gathered from several nations, and in a modest but significant way, by scholars at this University.

We are proud of McGill, placed in a strategic position within Canada at a time of grave decision concerning the future shape of this nation. If our original and probably most prestigious Faculty is that of Medicine, on the Humanities side a diverse collegium of scholars and teachers has similar excellence on record.

I have been asked to mention something of this record in regard to Kierkegaard research at McGill, and then to say something about the Kierkegaard-Malantschuk Collection.

I trust that you will maintain the concept of irony as you listen to a theologian. You recall Kierkegaard's own words, in a Journal entry (1850): "The 'theological professor' indicates a point of view in Christendom; from the way 'the professor' is judged one can see the status in Christendom and how Christianity is judged."

The fact is that the year 1950 marks a certain beginning of interest in Kierkegaard here. In the Department of Philosophy R. D. Maclennan was chairman, the staff seminar was on Kierkegaard, and a new appointee was the young Alastair McKinnon. Across campus in the Faculty of Divinity (as it was then called) James S. Thomson was Dean and, while certainly not a Kierkegaardian (whatever that might be), encouraged research in a way parallel to that of Maclennan. In 1954 he would state, "The new appreciation of Kierkegaard is not a revival, it is a discovery."

Perhaps this characterizes Kierkegaard research at McGill——a quest, an attempt to discover the true Kierkegaard. Those of us, whether in philosophy or in religious studies, who honour S. K. and think him worth attention, have profited from a common sense of the need to overcome caricature and to seek an evaluation based on evidence rather than preconception. This has been given programmatic definition by Alastair McKinnon, of course: to recover the "true" Kierkegaard from his "phantom" which continues to haunt academe.

Before turning to McKinnon I should note other names of our present researchers, particularly Walker and Khan in Philosophy and Carpenter and McLelland in Religious Studies. Perhaps Jeremy Walker should be specially singled out for his contribution to the ethical foundation at the heart of Kierkegaard's thought.

Who was the real Kierkegaard? Melancholy Dane, a kind of poet, psychologist, moralist, aesthete, irrationalist? Most obvious from the modern debate and writing is Malantschuk's title The Controversial Kierkegaard. Alastair McKinnon's research on S. K. began with the pseudonymous works, a bold and necessary step in solving the essential problem of authorship and identity. It was quite logical that about 1967 a second phase should take over, the Indices project. For the Kierkegaard Indices are a research tool, designed and honed by a master craftsman willing to undertake a massive and painstaking task on behalf of all of us who wish to test hypotheses and thus to let the authentic S. K. show himself.

About the four volumes of the Indices published between 1970 and 1975 N. J. Cappelørn has said, "there is no doubt that Professor McKinnon has ushered in a new phase of Kierkegaard research."

And now a third "stage on McKinnon's way" is on view. He has moved into a different focus for the programming technique mastered in preparing the Indices, the task of what is best called "conceptual topography." If McKinnon is the star of our McGill Kierkegaard researchers, indeed the pole star or lodestar for most of us, this phase represents perhaps his zenith as the most complex and important of problems are now under investigation. And this is a good sighting on which to end this first subject.

Turning now to the Kierkegaard-Malantschuk Collection, I think it good to say a word about how it came to McGill, for the record as it were. The characters involved in this story included Dr. Gregor Malantschuk, Mrs. Grethe Kjær, Alastair McKinnon and, later, Dr. H. P. Rohde and Dr. Hans Möller, both of whom were working in the Royal Library in Copenhagen many years ago when the Kierkegaard papers were being catalogued, and both of whom were involved in that work.

The story is a simple but interesting one. At the conclusion of the founding meeting of the Kierkegaard Academy in November 1977, Howard Hong and Alastair McKinnon visited their beloved and greatly respected mentor Gregor Malantschuk who at that time informed McKinnon that he wished to see him as soon as possible on a matter of some importance. Unfortunately, McKinnon was unable to return to Copenhagen until August 25, 1978, five days after Dr. Malantschuk's death. However, Mrs. Kjær knew the entire situation and, having checked with McKinnon, succeeded in persuading the Danish authorities to allow this precious collection to go to McGill in accordance with Dr. Malantschuk's expressed intention. Among the several factors involved in this decision, which in one sense has brought us together here today, was the high esteem in which Dr. Malantschuk held the Kierkegaard Indices and their editor.

You will see the collection for yourself shortly. You will meet some of those about whom I have spoken briefly. We hope you enjoy these and all aspects of this conference, that together our exploration of resources and results will encourage others to join us in the enterprise of Kierkegaard search and research.

2

THE KIERKEGAARD-MALANTSCHUK COLLECTION AS A BASIS FOR RESEARCH

H. P. Rohde

You remember the old saying that all roads lead to Rome. In the same way you might say that all roads lead to Søren Kierkegaard. Perhaps more than anyone else he has pondered the basic problems of life. Perhaps with more imagination than any other he has known how to represent the fundamental views of life and types or, as he called them, stages of existence. Further, and most important, more than any one else he has lived passionately in and for thinking; in splendid isolation, and mostly in violent opposition to his contemporaries. Not content simply to analyze the problems of life in all their shades and consider them to their utmost consequences, he further divided himself into individual author-personalities each with its own religious, psychological, philosophical, and stylistic individuality. His was an enormous production, and he could justly claim that it represented a literature within the entire body of literature.

Given the quantity and variety of Kierkegaard's writings and their complex relation to his own life, it is both understandable and natural that Kierkegaard research up until now has followed very many different paths and in the future will presumably continue to do so.

The first, most obvious, and ultimately the best way

to approach Kierkegaard is quite simply to read him. But even here there are great difficulties, at least if one wants to understand him correctly. This is partly due to the fact that his style is often heavy and intricate, especially when he uses the elaborate philosophical language of his time. It is also partly due to the fact that he often expresses himself indirectly by way of metaphors and parables. Finally, it is due to the strange enigmatic character of his writings and to his habit of speaking in riddles.

Søren Kierkegaard is in fact the great enigma of world literature. His need of communication was enormous, but so, apparently, was his need for mystification. Speaking of the works which he left behind, he maintained that no one would ever be able to "find any evidence of what has virtually filled my life."

Not surprisingly, the effort to obtain a right understanding and interpretation of Kierkegaard's writings has therefore sometimes led researchers to pursue roundabout ways, some of which turned out to be shortcuts and others perhaps simply wrong.

It may appear a little comical that treatises have been written about the pipes he smoked, the food he ate, the wine he drank, the rooms in which he lived, and the bookbinders which he used. Of course, it is indeed comical; but Kierkegaard is a magic circle, and once you have been placed inside that circle the usual ideas of what is great and what is not cease to be self-evident.

As we all know, genius itself has its own inexplicable magnetism. This is as true in the case of Kierkegaard as in that of other great personalities. First you study them simply for the sake of what they have done——whether as generals, politicians, or painters——but gradually the personality behind the work compels one's attention, drawing you away from this starting point and toward the rich peculiarities of the man himself. Think for example of Van Gogh's cutting off of his ear and all that it has contributed to the fame of this great painter, despite the fact that it has, of course, very little to do with the understanding of his art.

As already suggested, the genius behind the work has a tendency to become the main thing. At the same time we must admit that when a great personality is involved it is often difficult to draw the line between what is important and what is not. It is necessary to stress this because it is particularly true in the case of Søren Kierkegaard.

One of the many ways to study Kierkegaard is in terms of his relation to books. Today as we are gathered to inaugurate "The Kierkegaard-Malantschuk Collection" it seems natural to pursue this way a little further. However, here again it may prove difficult to determine what is essential and important. It is clear that the contents of his books were by far the most important to Kierkegaard, but it is important to remind the modern reader of mass-produced books that because of the circumstances of his time Kierkegaard was able to determine the outward appearance of at least some copies of his books and that he set great store by the quality of their printing and binding.

It is also perhaps necessary to remind the modern reader that the purely bibliographical side of Kierkegaard research began very early. Already in his own lifetime, in fact in 1847, the Dictionary of Danish Authors, edited by Th. H. Erslew, published a list of his writings. Here we find the following: "He is supposed to be the author of: Either/Or. A Fragment of Life, edited by Victor Eremita. I - II." It seems to me that this short remark provides a very revealing glimpse of the little provincial town which Copenhagen was at that time. You can almost hear the gossip of the Copenhageners wondering if this strange little dandified whipper-snapper of a man, who spent his days walking idly up and down the streets or talking in the coffee-houses, could really be the author of this colossus of a book!

Kierkegaard died on 11 November 1855, and already in April of the following year his book collection came under the auctioneer's hammer. The printed catalogue of the sale is a typical rush job and later became the subject of a number of sophistic discussions. But Kierkegaard researchers must be grateful for it as it is and remains the main source of our knowledge about the books which Kierkegaard owned. And despite the summary description of the books, Kierkegaard's marked bibliophile disposition shows through; for example, some of the items are described as "neat with gilt edges."

The auction was a tremendous sensation. People flocked to the place from far and near, and the books brought what a contemporary describes as "enormously high prices."

Younger academics and learned professors appeared as bidders, but many ordinary persons also turned up to acquire a book as a memento of the great man. Indeed, the sale was a symptom of the fame which, despite his isolation, Kierkegaard had gained within his native land even in his own lifetime.

Another indication from a different level of the high esteem in which Kierkegaard's contemporaries held his works is the collection of his newspaper articles which the Danish philosopher Rasmus Nielsen, in collaboration with the Rev. P. Chr. Zahle, published in 1857, only two years after his death. This book reprints almost all Kierkegaard's journalistic pieces and, as a supplement, almost all the articles written by others by way of reply. Furthermore, this book ends with a bibliography of all his writings, articles as well as books, which in respect to exactitude and thoroughness is unequalled within the whole of the Kierkegaard bibliographical literature. With but few exceptions, every book is described with its title, half-title, shorter or longer table of contents, the year and date of publication, and, in addition, the date when the actual printing was finished. I very much doubt that any such elaborate, complete, and accurate bibliography has ever appeared for any other author so shortly after his death.

It is very important to call attention to this book because it is surprisingly little known. Time and again I have talked with Kierkegaard researchers, Danish as well as foreign, who did not know and had never heard about it, and I am therefore very pleased to have this opportunity to make it better known.

This bibliographical masterpiece laid the foundation for the world-wide fame which was to come, but, as we know, it took a very long time. For Hans Christian Andersen it was much easier. This is hardly surprising since over his fairy tales might be written "To the happy many!" whereas over the heavy and melancholy works of Kierkegaard one might write "To the unhappy few!" At any rate, Kierkegaard <u>is</u> not and <u>will</u> never become an author for the masses.

Kierkegaard did not attain world-wide fame until after the last Great War. This was surely due more than anything else to the fact that the fashionable philosophy of that time borrowed its name from Kierkegaard's constant emphasis on the concept of existence. In any event, it was only then that Kierkegaard's name emerged into the limelight of the world stage, and only then that the time was ripe for that more special side of Kierkegaard research connected with his book collection and his relation to books in all their aspects.

Book prices are a good barometer of fame. I have myself witnessed the great difference in prices of original editions of Kierkegaard's own writings before and after the Second World War. In the 1930s, for instance, it was possible to buy at book sales the various collections of Kierkegaard's Discourses in the original edition at about fifty øre or half a Danish crown a piece. His main works were a little more expensive. I bought Stages on Life's Way for nine crowns and a nice copy of Either/Or for twenty-one!

It was quite different after the war. Both Kierkegaard's main works and the Discourses which book collectors had earlier despised quickly reached one hundred crowns, and prices continued to rise, this due in part, no doubt, to the fact that foreign collectors were now participating in the bidding. Sometimes second-hand booksellers announced complete sets of Kierkegaard's writings for sale. In the beginning such a set cost twenty to thirty thousand crowns, but in about 1970 a complete set was put up for sale at the price of nearly sixty thousand Danish crowns.

I have been interested in Kierkegaard from my early youth, but it was only in 1949 when I became a librarian at the Royal Library in Copenhagen that I was led to study more closely the problems concerning his book collection. At that time this was still an uncultivated field. For instance, to my great surprise I found that about fifty books bought by the library in the sale in 1856 still stood unheeded among the other ordinary books of the library and could be borrowed for outside use like any other books. One of my first tasks, therefore, was to register these books and have them incorporated in the Kierkegaard Archives. In the course of this work I discovered that these and other archives in the library contained much very rich material, including bookbinders' and booksellers' bills, which threw new light upon Kierkegaard as a book collector. On the basis of this material I was able to publish in 1961 a rather comprehensive treatise about Kierkegaard as a book collector which, besides incorporating previously unknown source material, including a list of books having belonged to Kierkegaard, tried to give a complete and well-rounded picture of Kierkegaard in this role.

This investigation clearly established that Kierkegaard had been a natural and very considerable book collector. Just as he could be tempted by the windows of the antique shops on his way through town, he also occasionally bought a book which he did not strictly need but to which he simply took a fancy. In a fragmentary note in his papers from 1836 he writes: "How many books have I not bought through a strange urge and left lying about until . . . . "

While Kierkegaard was interested in the contents of his books he also attached great importance to their outward appearance. From my investigation it appears that most of his books have been specially bound and often handsomely so. He treated his books very carefully, and we know that he sometimes had worn bindings repaired. Special copies of his own writings were printed on exquisite paper and in some cases specially bound. Incidentally, I was also able to establish that his favourite binder was N. C. Møller of Copenhagen.

Perhaps the most important conclusion of this study was that the sales catalogue does not give a very reliable impression of the size of his library. Surviving booksellers' bills clearly show that early in his life Kierkegaard owned considerably more books than appear in the catalogue. In brief, that catalogue shows only the books which he owned at the time of his death and not by any means all he had owned at one time or another during his life.

With regard to Kierkegaard's own reading, it is important to point out that he undoubtedly made great use of the different public libraries in Copenhagen. Certainly the notes in his own papers show that he has read many books other than those which were at one time or another in his collection.

The main purpose of studying Kierkegaard's library is that it provides the essential basis for our knowledge of his reading and of what might be called his literary horizon. However, a quite special interest attaches to the actual books which he has certainly owned. Those which have been preserved show not only what he has read or may have read, but also how he has read them; even which parts or single sentences have attracted his attention. Of course the titles of these works are important but so too are the marks and signs he has made during his reading.

Before we can take full advantage of these sources, it will be necessary first to determine and record all the books which Kierkegaard certainly owned and, as a next step, carry out a thorough investigation of his use of these books. At the moment, however, neither of these tasks is much more than begun. Many books which undoubtedly belonged to Kierkegaard show no sign of his reading, a fact which does not necessarily imply that he has not read them. However, some of his books show different marks on the pages ranging from broad "dogears" and small crosses to written notes of shorter or longer length. There is an important task of editing and deciphering to be done and one which, moreover, goes hand in hand with the editing of Kierkegaard's "Papers."

But how is it possible today to identify books which have actually belonged to Kierkegaard? It would of course have been much easier had he written his name in his books, but it appears that only very rarely did he do so. Here, however, we can get a great deal of help from a careful and detailed study of those books which have already been identified as having belonged to him. Thus, for example, we learn that he usually had his presentation copies bound in black glazed paper by his favourite bookbinder, both of which facts now emerge as of much more than mere bibliophile interest. Further, we can also gain from this same source a knowledge of his special way of marking and underlining the books he read which, of course, can also be of value in this connection.

Another extremely important and useful tool which can aid in the identification of books once belonging to Kierkegaard must be emphasized: this is the auctioneer's sales record of Kierkegaard's library. His books were sold during the days 8 to 10 April 1856. The sales record shows not only the prices of the books but also the names of the buyers.

Some of these buyers have inscribed their names in their new purchases together with some expression of delight at having acquired a book belonging to the famous man. But unfortunately this is not the general rule. This is no doubt connected with the fact that a large number of books were bought by booksellers for their own shops and consequently lack any such information about their origin. However, in those cases where the name in the book is the same as that found in the sales record there is a fair possibility that the book in question once belonged to Kierkegaard.

Because of these considerations, it was of great importance for Kierkegaard research that in 1967 the Royal Library in Copenhagen published an annotated edition of this sales record, including the text of the printed catalogue, the hand-written information of the sales record, and notes about books already identified as having belonged to Kierkegaard, together with an introduction in Danish and English about Kierkegaard as a book collector.

Kierkegaard's library comprised well over the two thousand books sold by auction in 1856. Of these books between sixty and seventy have now been identified at the Royal Library in Copenhagen and about another fifty in other public libraries in Denmark. A list of these books was published in 1966 in the Year Book of the Royal Library. In addition, many private collectors, Danes as well as foreigners, have acquired books from Kierkegaard's library in the years after the Second World War. All in all it may be estimated that at least two hundred books formerly owned by Kierkegaard are now identified as such. This is only approximately one-tenth of his whole library, but it might perhaps be wise to rest satisfied for the moment with this preliminary result. Certainly there is much evidence that it will be very difficult, and will become increasingly more difficult, to trace the still missing volumes.

On the other hand, interest in Kierkegaard's library is not and should not be limited to his own personal copies. From the point of view of research any copy of a book having belonged to Kierkegaard is of value regardless of whether that copy itself was once in his possession. Since the content of all copies of an edition is identical, any copy of the same edition as Kierkegaard's is of great importance.

Because of this fact there have been a number of energetic endeavours from various quarters to build up reconstructions of Kierkegaard's library, especially in the last twenty or thirty years. This has been going on not only in Denmark but also in other parts of the world, in America, for instance, as well as in Japan. In Copenhagen one must mention the so-called "Kierkegaard Library," established under the auspices of the Theological Faculty of the University of Copenhagen, which is already of considerable extent. Another great and valuable collection is that founded by Professor Hong and his wife in Northfield, Minnesota. And, last but not least, I mention the collection which we today are gathered to inaugurate and which is due to the energy and untiring efforts of the late Dr. Gregor Malantschuk.

A common and distinctive feature of all these collections is that from the beginning rather wide limits have been set for their size and scope. With few exceptions, all these collections follow the same general pattern. Original and later editions of Kierkegaard's own writings constitute the nucleus which is itself surrounded by circle after circle of other groups. The first are books which have belonged to Kierkegaard or which, according to the sales catalogue, correspond to books having belonged to him. The second are books not mentioned in the sales catalogue but which, according to other sources, are known to have belonged to him. The third are books which we know he has read, although perhaps not owned. In addition there is a still wider circle of books of earlier date or from his own time which for some reason or other may be related to his literary background or which serve in a general way to cast light upon his spiritual as well as his material environment. Last, and as a kind of appendix, there are the books dealing with his work and personality.

Dr. Gregor Malantschuk ranked high among the great book collectors of our time. He collected with unique energy and knowledge and in spite of the fact that he lived under very difficult economic circumstances. He was well aware that he collected in competition with time and that the books he sought were coveted by many other collectors, each seeking books relevant to the famous authors of his own special interest. Here it must be remembered that German literature, fictional as well as philosophical and theological, loomed large in Kierkegaard's library, and that, because many German book collections were destroyed during the war, Danish antiquarian book shops were virtually drained of German books by purchasers from Germany in the years immediately following. It was in fact at the last moment that Dr. Malantschuk took the initiative. Today it would be very difficult, if not impossible, to gather a collection of this standard.

It has been my fortune to follow the creation of Dr. Malantschuk's collection at rather close range. One day in 1961, shortly after I had published my treatise on Kierkegaard as a book collector and when I was working in the Royal Library, I received a message that a gentleman was waiting in the entrance hall and wanted to speak to me. It was Dr. Malantschuk. He told me about his interest in Kierkegaard and asked whether he might be allowed to see the books from his library.

Seldom have I met so friendly, so polite, and so modest a man. He was very glad to see what I could show him, and when he told me that he himself was a collector of Kierkegaard and that he believed that he was in possession of books which had belonged to him, our first meeting was soon followed by others. It was not long before I realized that here was a quite extraordinary collector. Every time I saw him the rows of his books had grown and at last they filled the walls in his small flat from floor to ceiling and the shelves had spread over the floor scarcely leaving room to sit down.

It was a great pleasure to talk with Dr. Malantschuk. He was a very genial and good-humoured man. In addition, he had mastered the Danish language surprisingly well. He was born in the Ukraine and, though coming to Denmark rather late in life, nevertheless acquired an admirable familiarity with the Danish way of talking. He spoke absolutely correctly with only a slight accent and could play upon the finer shades of the language, especially when there was a joke to be made.

For the most part our conversations had their basis in our respective purchases and would often turn upon the question whether one of them could possibly have belonged to Kierkegaard. But from here to the problems in Kierkegaard's writings the leap was not very long. With gratitude I recall his ability to explain difficult passages and all the stimulation and encouragement he has given me to pursue my own special studies. It is rare to meet people who unite so much learning with so much warm-hearted humanity as did Dr. Malantschuk. I cherish the memory of this splendid man.

In conclusion I want to congratulate McGill University upon acquiring Dr. Malantschuk's Kierkegaard library. There is no doubt that, so long as our traditional Western civilization stands, this library will maintain its reputation as one of the most prominent and most valuable collections of its kind. Certainly it should have a high place as an eminent and important resource for solving the many problems still remaining in Kierkegaard research.

Our time has witnessed a tendency to advocate the restoring of works of art and other treasures to their original homelands. It seems to me that this is a sad and mistaken consequence of patriotism. For my part, I think that a country becomes greater when its works of art and literature are spread widely over the earth. In my eyes it is an honour to Denmark that McGill University has sought and accepted responsibility for this collection which, having come all the long way from Copenhagen to Montreal, now stands here to serve the study of a great Danish thinker and author. As I see it, it is a further confirmation of what Hans Christian Andersen, Kierkegaard's friend and fellow-countryman, wrote more than a hundred years ago in his beautiful poem to Denmark:

> a small country, and yet so far on earth
> still is heard the Danish song and chiselblow.

Or, as these lines read in Danish:

> et lille land, og dog saa vidt paa Jorden
> end høres Danskens Sang og Mejselslag.

3

THE AVAILABILITY OF THE KIERKEGAARD-MALANTSCHUK COLLECTION

Hans Möller

It is a matter of great pride to McGill University to have acquired the Malantschuk Collection of Kierkegaard books. It is particularly so since this is the first time a major Kierkegaard collection has left Denmark.

It is a matter of equal pride to me to have been associated with the acquisition of this Kierkegaard collection. For me it is a circle completed since as a young librarian I used to work with the Kierkegaard Archives in the Royal Library a long time ago. A close collegial relationship between Professor Alastair McKinnon and myself allowed me to give a helping hand in acquiring the collection for McGill. We know that Dr. Gregor Malantschuk wanted his collection to go to the McGill Libraries after his death and this as a result of his own intimate professional relationship with Professor McKinnon.

The McGill Libraries have long had a fairly decent collection of books by and about Søren Kierkegaard designed to support already existing Kierkegaard studies at McGill. Several scholars at our university have been very active in this field, and it was only natural that we wished to take advantage of this unique opportunity to enlarge our collection and make McGill a significant centre for studies of this great philosopher.

The Director of Libraries, Marianne Scott, gave immediate promise of financial support for the purchase, aided by a generous grant from the Social Sciences and Humanities Research Council of Canada. Equally enthusiastic support was accorded by Alison Cole, the area librarian responsible for the McLennan Library, where the collection will be housed in the Department of Rare Books and Special Collections, under the guidance of its head, Elizabeth Lewis. Both colleagues of mine are here today and anxious to give you a first glimpse of the collection itself.

Before we take a look at the collection, allow me to describe it briefly. It consists of 1,000 volumes in very good physical condition, including a complete collection of first editions of Kierkegaard's works. Secondly, it includes a partial reconstruction of Kierkegaard's private study library as it was at the time of his death. Six books are in fact his own copies while the rest came from other sources in the same editions that he possessed. As well, the collection includes a number of important books written by Kierkegaard's contemporaries and other books he is assumed to have read.

I am not myself a Kierkegaard scholar, but it is easy to be enthusiastic about such a marvellous collection gathered by Dr. Malantschuk over a period of many years and no doubt as a result of painstaking search and personal sacrifice. As a librarian I feel proud to have been instrumental in bringing the collection here. In fact, I went to Copenhagen and visited Dr. Malantschuk's home, where Mrs. Kjær showed me the books. And I helped arrange the shipment across the ocean, while Dr. Rohde supervised the actual packing of the books. Fortunately, all arrived safely and fairly quickly here at McGill.

It is indeed a classical example of one of the most positive actions a librarian can perform——to work as a member of a team between faculty and library staff, all in an effort to facilitate research. Many of you may have an image of librarians as persons who never read a book and who see their main function in life as that of preventing other potential readers from doing so. Perhaps some professors and students feel we do everything we can to make matters more complicated. I hope that this is no longer the case, if it ever was. As I have said, I feel very proud of having helped to get the collection here, and I know that my library colleagues share this sense of pride.

Indeed, nothing can demonstrate this better than the fact that this Kierkegaard collection is presently being fully catalogued according to the Library of Congress classification. Further, the cataloguing data will be included in McGill's automated cataloguing file. Share-access to this file will make the records accessible to Canadian and international scholars.

It is exactly these new methods in library science, especially computer-based cataloguing, that enables us librarians now to make collections more accessible to scholars. It is one of the many important factors that make it possible for librarians to play a role of partnership in research.

I wish to assure you that McGill University Libraries take very seriously the responsibility of possessing this valuable collection, and that we will do everything possible to facilitate access by all of you to the Kierkegaard-Malantschuk Collection. The significance of these books is emphasized by the presence here of so many distinguished scholars from Denmark, U.S.A., and Canada.

Last fall when I visited Copenhagen and had occasion to discuss the McGill acquisition of the collection, I found that my colleagues there welcomed this effort to spread resources on Søren Kierkegaard outside Denmark, thus encouraging studies on an international scale. McGill has made a serious commitment to become an important centre for such research and studies in North America. Please be assured that McGill will honour this commitment.

4

THE RETROSPECTIVE UNDERSTANDING OF SØREN KIERKEGAARD'S TOTAL PRODUCTION

Niels Jørgen Cappelørn

When I was asked to speak at this conference, my first thought was to talk about Kierkegaard's Efterladte Papirer, the journals and papers left behind after his death. I considered this most appropriate to the theme of this conference "Kierkegaard: Resources and Results." Of course, my first response to the request to give a lecture here was one of delight and honour, and I would like to say at the outset how pleased I am to be here.[1]

Of the many good reasons to choose Kierkegaard's Journals as my subject, the most important is the fact that a very extensive selection of these papers has recently been published in English by Howard and Edna Hong. However, I finally rejected this idea since the result could very easily become too historical and technical and thus possibly irrelevant to the purpose of the conference. Therefore, and with Alastair McKinnon's approval, I decided instead to utilize the Journals themselves; not to talk about them, but actually to use them as practical sources. Hence in this lecture I set myself the following task: using the Journals and related writings about the authorship as sources, to attempt to present an integrated understanding of Kierkegaard's total literary production which, moreover, accounts for its total design. In doing so I will concern myself with two theses:

1. The Journals are not independent of the entire production but constitute a part of it.
2. A complete understanding of the entire production can be obtained only through a retrospective process of interpretation.

A conventional method of examining an author's production, whether philosophical, literary, or theological, is to build upon biography, bibliography, and then reflective analysis—a form of commentary which presupposes consideration of both biographical data and the author's actual writings. Unfortunately, in addition to being tedious and hackneyed, this approach labours under a great misconception since it assumes that the author's life and literary activity must be rigidly determined by a kind of inward necessity in both his heredity and environment. There is no recognition that the irrational can sweep in and leave its indelible mark on the development of an author and his ideas.

It is particularly inappropriate to employ such a method in Kierkegaard's case. Here we confront an author and an authorship profoundly determined by the irrational which Kierkegaard himself interpreted as the intervention and assistance of "Governance," that is, of God. As we shall see, and as Kierkegaard himself understood it, his authorship was in the service of the truth and in obedience to Governance and its commands. Understood in this way, the whole of his literary activity becomes at once both a collaboration with and an act of worship of God.

When we experience an artist's work, for example, when in the theatre we follow a play's development from beginning to end, we participate in a series of events until all its details, like the pieces of a mosaic, finally fall into place and produce a whole, thus giving us an integrated understanding of the entire piece. In Kierkegaard's expression, we live through the piece forwards while understanding it backwards or retrospectively.

In a journal entry Kierkegaard remarked about himself: "I am nothing but pure reflection: backwards."[2] Paraphrased a bit this means that Kierkegaard constantly reflected upon his life and authorship as it progressed but only understood the whole by considering it after it had occurred and was behind him. He formulated it thus in the postscript to his short piece On My Work as an Author: "Now I understand it in its totality; I have not from the beginning been able thus to take it all in; this process has also constituted my own education."[3]

As late as March 1855, only a half year before his death, Kierkegaard exclaimed in his journals: "The longer I live the more I am convinced that I have a demon, an ideality. Because of it I have never related to myself directly, whatever the relationship. The relationship has always been as follows: I am the one who has spent my strength on creating difficulties and obstacles for myself, to which I then related myself. Often I have not been aware that I did so, and not till later realized that this was the case."[4]

Put together with other expressions of a similar nature, these entries suggest that Kierkegaard understood his life and work quite differently in retrospect than he did as the events and writing transpired as a stream before him. More precisely, in retrospect Kierkegaard interpreted his life and work _from a religious point of view._ He states it this way in the journals: "what always . . . takes precedence, the solicitude of Governance, which accounts for the fact that I always understand best backwards."[5] And a little later: "That I constantly go backwards is an expression, a qualitative expression for 'Fear and Trembling.'"[6] For Kierkegaard "Fear and Trembling" is always a religious concept which expresses a self-denying fear of God. Given these considerations, I consider the phrase "_to live forwards, but to understand backwards_" as a key to the understanding of Kierkegaard's life and as a hermeneutic principle for the interpretation of his work and thought.

The second half of the statement "to understand backwards or retrospectively," first appears in Kierkegaard's early work _From the Papers of One Still Living_ as an expression attributed to Carl Daub. Here Kierkegaard maintains that there should be a moment in existence when "Life is understood backwards, through the Ideal."[7] Only thus can one attain that view of life which leads everything back to the Ideal. This was precisely what Kierkegaard believed Hans Christian Andersen lacked, and this was why he made him the target of this early piece. In Kierkegaard's eyes, Andersen had no unifying principle, no plan for his literary activity, only a sort of kaleidoscope of ideas.

At the end of 1843 Kierkegaard again took up this expression and with the Daub statement in mind wrote in his journal: "Philosophy is perfectly right in saying that life must be understood backwards. But then one forgets the other clause—that it must be lived forwards. The more one thinks through this clause, the more one concludes that life in temporality never becomes properly understandable, simply because never at any time does one get perfect repose to take a stance: Backwards."[8] This quote, placed together with the one already mentioned, shows how Kierkegaard could seize a philosophical expression and transform it into an existential religious category in which the academic-philosophical content was subordinated and the existential significance emphasized.

With an authorship of the substance and dimensions of Kierkegaard's it is an enormous help to have the author's own description and overview of how he wanted his work to be understood. Fortunately we have such an account in Kierkegaard's own journals in which he clearly indicates that his life and work are to be understood "backwards." I therefore hold that this is a legitimate way, indeed the only legitimate way, of interpreting Kierkegaard, namely, to proceed from his own writings about the authorship and then attempt with him to live forwards and understand backwards through the various works in order to understand his production as a whole.

Precisely this same retrospective approach is found in the very first pages of Kierkegaard's own reflective piece On My Work as an Author from 1851: "When considered as a whole, the authorship is religious from first to last."[9] It was quite difficult for Kierkegaard to produce such a synthetic "Accounting" of his literary production, and when he had completed it he observed in his journals: "The small book On My Work as an Author is an abbreviation and, considering the extent of the authorship, even a very brief abbreviation. One word, one comma in it sometimes represents very comprehensive expositions. It may even be said to need a commentary . . . ."[10] Kierkegaard has provided such a commentary, indeed a very comprehensive commentary, partly in the journals and partly in his book The Point of View for my Work as an Author, which he decided should be published only posthumously.

During his own lifetime Kierkegaard published only the very concentrated work On My Work as an Author (1851). I will say more about this piece later, but before doing so I want to discuss a second and equally important source, or resource, for the understanding of Kierkegaard as a religious author and of his authorship's religious integrity, namely, his journals, many of which are now available in English.

In a certain sense Walter Lowrie was right when he claimed in his Kierkegaard biography that the journals are not really diaries. But he was only partially correct when he argued his claim as follows: "We speak properly of 'The Diary of the Seducer' and of the diary of the young man in 'Guilty/Not Guilty?' where the element of time was essential, but the entries in Kierkegaard's journals were timeless, they were the records of his thoughts, things he wanted to remember, some of them thoughts he would ultimately use in his writings, very few of them being essentially related to particular dates, and few of them actually dated during the first years."[11] Now it is true that Kierkegaard's journals were not diaries in the ordinary sense. But the reason is not, as Lowrie maintains, that they are timeless. On the contrary, they were historically situated and shaped and very much determined by time. Indeed, many of the entries are often precise responses to particular books, scholarly journals, and newspapers which he had read. It is therefore enormously important for Kierkegaard scholars to have access to his library, in order to know what books he owned and which he read.

The entries can also be descriptions of concrete events or reflections on actual observations Kierkegaard made during his regular walks through the streets of Copenhagen. When such events and observations passed through his fantasy-filled mind, their eventual description in the journals often far exceeded the original or actual circumstances. Indeed, quite often Kierkegaard would build upon these events or observations in order to point up fundamental linkages and connections in human existence. Sometimes the entries are also continuations of discussions Kierkegaard had in the course of the day with leading figures in Copenhagen's intellectual circles or with ordinary people. (Such encounters with ordinary folk, especially with those from the lower class, were extremely important for Kierkegaard.) The entries could also be reactions to last Sunday's sermon, and in such cases even an insignificant remark by a preacher might unleash a virtual torrent of important theological considerations.

Again, entries in his journals could be closely connected with Kierkegaard's planning and rough drafts for a book. Here he would often register his spontaneous thoughts and later link them together. The entries clearly reflect his struggles with definitions and the connecting of concepts, all of them preliminary to his final writing of a book. The journal entries therefore provide us with valuable insight into Kierkegaard's actual working procedures. They are often rehearsals of ideas and expressions before their final appearance in a published work.

Furthermore, the journal entries can often assist us in sketching out the history of a particular work. In many cases we can trace its development from the jotting down of its first rough ideas through his struggles with the details and problems of its structure all the way through to the entry in which the final shape of the work is settled and the decision to publish is taken. This final stage was reached, as many entries indicate, only after protracted considerations on Kierkegaard's part. Often he would waver, decide, change his mind, decide again. He would also draft replies to polemical reviews or critical discussions of his books in other publications, especially when he believed he could or would be misunderstood. For example, Rasmus Nielsen's camouflaged plagiarism of passages from Philosophical Fragments and Concluding Unscientific Postscript gave rise to a stream of extremely bitter entries which at the same time contain an extraordinarily precise formulation of Kierkegaard's view of the relationship between doubt and faith.

These entries are therefore invaluable sources for understanding many of Kierkegaard's concepts and their development. By referring to the entries dealing with the production of a particular book it is often possible to trace the work much further back from its finished form to Kierkegaard's first groping efforts to delimit its themes or concepts. Such a procedure is often particularly helpful in unravelling the often very difficult formulations he uses in his published works. Because they are so frequently historical, his journal entries often reveal exactly how much Kierkegaard was influenced by external circumstances such as the reading of a particular book which perhaps only later found its way into his personal library and conceptual universe.

I will mention only one example of this, namely, Kierkegaard's discovery and working out of his famous concept of 'the leap.' Kierkegaard received the first impulse in this connection when he read Leibniz's Theodicee in Gottsched's 1763 edition. In an entry he noted: "Leibniz makes the very important observation S 212 that there are great difficulties involved in the inference of quality from quantity, just as from equals to similars."[12] About a year later Kierkegaard again took up this line of thought, reaching a provisional clarification after reading three of Trendelenburg's writings, while at the same time also being occupied with Lessing's work. With respect to Trendelenburg on the concept of the leap he wrote:

> Basic principles can be demonstrated only indirectly (negatively). This idea is frequently found and developed in Trendelenburg's Logische Untersuchungen. It is significant to me for the leap, and to show that the ultimate can be reached only as a limit . . . .
>
> By analogy and induction the conclusion can be reached only by a LEAP.
>
> All other conclusions are essentially tautological.
>
> Trendelenburg does not seem to be aware of the leap.[13]

After Kierkegaard had gone through Trendelenburg's Erlauterungen zu den Elementen der aristotelischen Logik and after he had read and underlined important passages in Elementa Logices Aristoteleae, he wrote:

> Trendelenburg resorts all too frequently to examples from mathematics and the natural sciences. Regrettably one finds almost no examples of the ethical in logic, which arouses in my thought a suspicion about logic and serves to support my theory of the leap, which is essentially at home in the realm of freedom, even though it ought to be metaphorically suggested in logic and should not be explained away, as Hegel does.[14]

About the same time Kierkegaard wrote the following about Lessing with regard to the leap; this in a draft of what later became Philosophical Fragments: "Lessing uses the word leap; whether it is an expression or a thought is a matter of indifference—I understand it as a thought."[15]

Here Kierkegaard was referring to volume VI of Lessing's Sämmtliche Schriften. He had all of the above mentioned books in his library and the first of them, Leibniz's Theodicee, in Gottsched's edition, was also in Gregor Malantschuk's library. It is here now in McGill as an important background source for Kierkegaard research. This example is quite representative and the entries cited reveal the extent to which Kierkegaard was capable of raising himself above a particular point to tackle far broader constellations of literary, philosophical, and theological ideas.

There is often a sense of soaring flight and a great freshness to these entries both with respect to their language and conceptual formulation. Kierkegaard himself often remarked upon this point:

> . . . . it would be good, through frequent re-writing, to let the thoughts come forth with the umbilical cord of the original mood, and to forget as much as possible all regards for their possible use, which would not happen in any case by referring to my journals; rather, by expectorating myself as in a letter to an intimate friend, I gain the possibility of self-knowledge and, in addition, fluency in writing, the same articulateness in written expression which I have to some extent in speaking, the knowledge of many little traits to which I have given no more than a quick glance, and finally, the advantage, if what Hamann says is true in another sense, that there are ideas which a man gets only once in his life. Such practice backstage is certainly necessary for every person who is not so gifted that his development is in some way public.[16]

There is a further important point to be made about the journal entries. Although the external circumstance which set a line of thought in motion was often of a purely personal and private character, Kierkegaard was nevertheless almost always able to see and deal with the universal human issues involved. Thus he consistently extracted the universal from his own life and milieu. To put the same point in a slightly different way, he lived and experienced his life forwards in order to understand and describe the universal backwards, that is, retrospectively. The journals show that Kierkegaard always wrote out of himself and his own experiences and that he constantly reached forward to describe the universal on the basis of the particular. Therefore I can agree with Lowrie that Kierkegaard's journals are not diaries in the usual sense. However, the correct basis for this claim is not that the journals are timeless, which they most definitely are not, but that they are a kind of literature.

Kierkegaard had a rather pronounced tendency to treat his experiences and observations in a literary or poetic manner. Indeed, his handling of the historical is quite often shaped by his urge to poeticize. He was always more concerned with the intellectual dimension and significance of a particular situation than with its purely objective historical details. Thus he often provided rather free accounts of episodes he was describing. For example, and as he himself said, he mixed in "something poetic" with the historical and chronological account of his engagement entitled "My Relationship to Her." Investigation shows that the historical elements in Kierkegaard's accounts are usually fairly reliable, but his main concern was with the interpretation of events, and this, of course, is naturally subjective. Thus one must exercise great caution and a critical sense in the use of the journals, not so much when they are employed as sources for the understanding of his conceptual universe as when utilized for tracing his biography. This granted, I believe that the journals are without doubt our most important source for the understanding of Kierkegaard's own view of himself and, together with The Point of View for My Work as an Author, the most valuable source for comprehending how he himself wanted his work to be understood.

In this connection I should like to emphasize that though Kierkegaard's journals are really part of his literary production and not simply diaries in the ordinary sense, this does not mean that they are spun out poetically, merely as inventive fiction or deception. As events occurred sequentially, that is forward for Kierkegaard, each had its own independent significance for his life and development. However, as he reflected backwards over them in order to understand their interconnections, they began to take on new significance for the authorship. In fact, they became one with his thinking and poetic creativity. Kierkegaard was quite clear about this himself and discussed this problem in an entry of 13 October 1853 with the title About Myself:

> No doubt some creativity still slipped into what I jotted down about myself in the journals of 1848 and 1849. It is not so easy to keep such a thing out when one is as poetically creative as I am. It appears the minute I pick up my pen. Strangely enough, in my inner being, I am much clearer and much more concise about myself. But as soon as I want to put it in writing, it promptly becomes a creative process. Similarly it is also strange that I have no desire to put down the religious impressions, ideas, and expressions which I myself use; they seem to be too important for that. Of these I have a few—but I have produced quantities of them. But only when such a phrase seems to have been consumed, as it were, can I think of jotting it down or letting it slip into what I write.[17]

In fact, there was such a close connection between Kierkegaard's personality and his authorship that these cannot be understood in isolation from each other. Kierkegaard was aware of this and remarked: "The time will come when not only my writings but my whole life, the intriguing secret of the whole machinery, will be studied and studied."[18]

Kierkegaard's earliest entries are mainly notes and brief recapitulations but those from the time he was being tutored in Schleiermacher's theology are broader and more independent formulations. In these he concerned himself particularly with the problem of predestination, and these early entries, from the last half of 1836, are really the best sources for an understanding of Kierkegaard's solution of this basic theological problem. Incidentally, a very clear account of this can be found in the first chapter of Gregor Malantschuk's important book Kierkegaard's Thought, translated by the Hongs.

Kierkegaard often used the journals for intellectual experimentation. Frequently over the space of days, occasionally weeks, and sometimes even months, he would attempt to think through a particular point of view with respect to some specific problem, including its different aspects and its furthest consequences. This approach is very typical of Kierkegaard and is evident throughout his entire authorship. Usually such reflections would begin as staccato-like utterances, later appear as an intellectual synthesis leading to real clarification, and finally emerge as finished statements which could be used, as they often were, in his published works.

Parallel with such entries, there gradually appeared a number of others entitled "de se ipso" or "concerning myself." In these Kierkegaard probed his own soul, his relation to the authorship and, particularly, the latter's connections and significance. It is thus appropriate to consider The Point of View for My Work as an Author as the work in which Kierkegaard actually began the publication of his journals.

The entries from the early years are particularly important because they serve as sources for an understanding of the formative years during which he absorbed impressions and knowledge for his later literary work. This is also the period in which his own view of life and his most important ideas were formed and in which his language found its characteristic form and style. The journal entries contain a great variety of genres, from straightforward diary-like jottings to efforts to define concepts, notes, aphorisms, excerpts from readings, literary drafts, ideas and plans for essays, and entire texts of books, sermons, edifying discourses, and so on.[19]

I must emphasize again, however, that the journals are really more a part of Kierkegaard's literary activity than actual diaries as such. In the foreword to his edition of the journals (1869-72) the editor H. P. Barfod characterized them in the following manner: "The Journals give the impression of having been developed as a partial digression from Kierkegaard's literary activity, as a medium for the deceased recluse's compulsion to intellectually discharge his ideas and feelings." Two points in this quotation are significant:

1. Kierkegaard thought through and attained clarity concerning his own ideas by writing them out and appears to have derived much benefit from doing so. He expressed this in the following: "Only when I am writing do I feel just fine."[20] "To write was my life."[21] "A deep depression has been kept down by writing."[22] Plainly, then, the journals are an important part of his literary production, which brings us to the other point.
2. The journals are parallel with and counterpart to the actual authorship and hence an important part of Kierkegaard's overall literary production. The nature of this complex and important relation is indicated more fully in the schema shown at the end of the present study.

The journals were "backstage practices" or "warm-ups" and as such important intellectual and literary exercises. In them the factual, as the existentially experienced, is transformed into thought and poetry which in turn refers back to the factual or existential life in concrete activity and responsible decision. The journals are therefore not completely private writings as diaries usually are.

Many entries reveal indirectly both in form and content that Kierkegaard wrote his journals with a possible reader in mind. Indeed, it was his idea that the journals should be published after his death, a fact which of course supports the view that they should be regarded as a part of his literary production. To this end he arranged and organized the various entries, provided identifying letters and subsection numbers, and even considered the matter of an appropriate title. In an entry from 1849 he wrote: "If someone wanted to publish my journals after my death, it could be done under the title: The Book of the Judge."[23]

Our second source, The Point of View for My Work as an Author, consists of an introduction and a principal portion subdivided into two sections, each composed of several chapters. To these Kierkegaard added an epilogue, an addendum entitled "The Single Individual, Two Notes Regarding My Activity as an Author" and, finally, a "Postscript." Clearly, this is a work of intricate if not ingenious design.

I would now like to undertake a more detailed analysis of the various parts of this work, paying particular attention to the principal ideas relevant to the line of inquiry already indicated. Of course, my main concern is to bring out the relationship of this particular work to the rest of the authorship. Kierkegaard himself called the internal relationship of the works "the authorship's movement," and it is essential for our purposes to understand this movement clearly. This can be accomplished if we proceed backwards, moving retrospectively through the authorship, realizing that it also had a normal forward pattern of development.

Before pursuing this course of inquiry, we must take a momentary glance at the journals in order to examine the history of this work. It appears from certain entries that Kierkegaard had begun a draft early in 1848. Gradually the scattered fragments began to take shape, and the work was finally completed later that year. At this point, however, Kierkegaard decided not to publish it because he thought it contained too much personal material. Hence it remained a part of the journals and was published only after his death.

From this point on Kierkegaard decided to devote his efforts to working on the draft of what he would call "a little piece about my authorship." This small book of only sixteen pages, later to be entitled On My Work as an Author, was in reality an extremely brief and concentrated version of the earlier work already mentioned and is now usually published with it.

In 1849 Kierkegaard decided to publish this second

shorter piece, not so much out of real inclination as a sense of obligation to his reader. He felt that his silence had to be broken by a clear and powerful statement of his intentions as an author. But he did not express himself so strongly as he had in the draft of The Point of View in the introduction of which he wrote: "In my work as an author I have now reached a point at which it is possible . . . once and for all as directly and openly as possible to explain what is what, what I as an author say I am."[24] What was the point Kierkegaard had reached in his authorship at this particular time? And why was this such a decisive moment for him? There appear to be two possible explanations:

1. The ground had been prepared in Kierkegaard's own life and milieu for a direct explanation of his authorship's overall unity and purpose, and he thought it possible that such an explanation could now be understood.
2. At this point Kierkegaard had also to confront the printing of the second edition of Either/Or which brought him into direct contact with the very beginning of the authorship. His production was undergoing a kind of repetition, one which he believed required an explanation.

But why permit such a repetition especially in view of the fact that he had allowed Constantine Constantius, the pseudonymous author of the aesthetic work Repetition to say, albeit half ironically, that there could be no repetition? Closer inspection reveals that a provisional answer is already given in this same book. In his last letter to Constantine Constantius the book's other main figure, "the young man," comes to the realization that there can be a repetition after all. But, it is important to note, this is an intellectual, i.e., an aesthetic-poetic rather than a concrete repetition. Further, it is undertaken only because of the young man's poetic propensity and is therefore a retrogressive or backward repetition.

A somewhat similar idea, but one on a qualitatively higher plane, is presented by another pseudonymous author, Johannes de Silentio, in Fear and Trembling. In this book an aesthetic-religious repetition is illustrated in terms of the Abraham story or legend. In this account Abraham receives his son Isaac back again, and thereby receives himself back doubly; all of this exclusively by the power of faith. Unlike that of "the young man," Abraham's repetition is concrete; it is undertaken by the power of faith and is thus a forward or progressive repetition. Here a movement has occurred, not just in the intellectual sphere, but in the religious as well.

The repetition within the authorship begun with the publication of the second edition of Either/Or was also a religious movement. It was not determined by any poetic impulse but by Kierkegaard's obedience to God's commands. According to Kierkegaard's own explanation of the relationship between his abilities as a poet and his poetic production, he was only a tool in God's hands.

Kierkegaard overflowed with both ideas and deep feelings. He had the ability of phantasy, of being able to imagine himself into other peoples' lives and situations. He had the dialectical ability to think through ideas and themes clearly and to their furthest consequences. (According to the undoubtedly autobiographical journal piece Johannes Climacus or, De omnibus dubitandum est, he had developed these abilities as a child with the assistance of his father.) However, Kierkegaard remained convinced that in using these abilities he must always follow God's commands. In this connection it is interesting to note that as the motto for The Point of View he chose the fifth verse of Brorson's hymn, "Op al den ting, som Gud har gjort" (Rise up, all of God's creation). That verse runs as follows:

> What shall I say? My words alone
> Do not express my duty.
> O God, how great thy wisdom is
> Thy goodness, might and beauty.[25]

Kierkegaard could scarcely have chosen a better motto. Brorson's lines clearly express in religious terms Kierkegaard's own conviction that his words would have been without significance had they been only of his own planning and creation. He believed that his writing was significant only if God spoke through him; only when, in obedience to God's commands, he expressed what God had required of him. In short, Kierkegaard saw his authorship as obedience to God and thus as an act of worship.

This perception can also be expressed in different but equally important terms. Kierkegaard saw his literary production as a linking together of necessity and freedom, terms which he saw as standing in an internal, dialectical relationship to one another. At the same moment as the necessity and obligation of God's commands are realized, freedom is also realized. Indeed, he saw the whole of his authorship as having been freely undertaken in response to God's will.

This same perception also explains Kierkegaard's willingness to permit a repetition within his authorship. This too he saw as obedience to God's command. This is the answer to the question: Why did Kierkegaard permit this repetition? It also corrects the expression "permitted himself." For Kierkegaard permitted himself to repeat because he understood it as something God wanted him to do. Likewise he felt himself compelled to explain in the form of direct communication the re-issuing of Either/Or as due not to his own wishes and feelings but as obedience to God. All this had to be explained openly and directly lest the reader see it as poetic self-assertion rather than as religious obligation.

Nevertheless Kierkegaard hesitated to publish even the short piece On My Work as an Author. Indeed, before he could send the book to the printer in 1851 he had first to supplement it with an addendum in which he defined yet more precisely his position as a religious author. Probably he was also afraid, as always, of making mistakes and of the consequences which might follow.

Some of Kierkegaard's hesitation is reflected in the journals. He reiterated that it had always been his desire to become a country pastor and it now looked as if this was finally possible since he was for the most part finished with his work as an author. He had taken an important turn. He had directly argued that as a Christian one could not dismiss the "demand to be a Christian," a demand he let the pseudonym Anti-Climacus "raise to the level of the highest ideal."[26] That demand had to be stated, to be put out in the open, instead of merely making the "admission" that one was not a Christian. Such an admission could easily result in a mere confession, which he saw as really a misuse of grace. This line of thought was emphasized in Training in Christianity, written in 1848 but first published in September 1851.

As late as 1851 Kierkegaard wrote in the journals: "It is therefore quite desirable for me that I am essentially done with my work as an author; a very little piece on 'my activity as an author,' which has lain here for about two years, will now perhaps be published."[27]

Here we have the causes prompting Kierkegaard to set forth his retrospective account of the authorship. First, the authorship was essentially complete. Second, he now confronted the publication of the second edition of Either/Or. As we have seen, this necessitated a repetition and demanded a straightforward explanation of the entire authorship's inner structure, of the relationship of the individual works to each other, and of the movement they had followed.

The movement of the authorship was, according to Kierkegaard's own account, "from the Poet——from the aesthetic, from Philosophy——from the speculative to the suggestion of the most inward determination of the Christian: from the pseudonymous Either/Or through the Concluding Unscientific Postscript with my name as editor, to The Discourses at the Communion on Friday and Training in Christianity."[28]

As indicated, Kierkegaard began his production as an aesthetic author or philosophical poet. Gradually he moved more in the direction of the speculative, only to appear, in the Concluding Unscientific Postscript, as a definitely religious thinker. But the process of ascent was not yet finished at this point. It continued as a constantly rising movement from "Religiousness A" to "Religiousness B" up toward an ever clearer determination of the Christian. It was at this point that Kierkegaard appeared as a truly religious author.

It is important to note that, according to Kierkegaard, a religious author is without authority. He repeated this constantly in order to make it clear that he was not an apostle but only one gifted with great ability. Between a genius and an apostle there is, as he put it, not just a quantitative but an absolute qualitative difference. His task as a religious author was, put briefly, "to make others aware, but without authority."

Before proceeding to trace the movement of the authorship further we must pause and glance back in order to examine the arrangement of the individual works and their relationship to one another. By doing so we can obtain a clearer understanding of Kierkegaard's insistence that the authorship was, in a way, ambiguous and duplicitous from the start.

The authorship's individual works can be divided into three principal groups. The first group consists of the aesthetic works from Either/ Or up to Stages on Life's Way and the explicitly religious works now generally known as

Edifying Discourses which appeared alongside them. The second part consists only of the Postscript which is not "an aesthetic work, and not a religious work, strictly speaking."[29] This work is also written under a pseudonym but, in contrast to the purely aesthetic works, was published in Kierkegaard's own name. The third group, consisting mainly of purely religious works, contains all the writings from Edifying Discourses in Various Spirits up to and including Two Discourses at the Communion on Friday. This third part also includes the little aesthetic article, "The Crisis and a Crisis in the Life of an Actress," under the pseudonym Inter et Inter.

We can see, therefore, how the early pseudonymous works written before the Postscript entwined themselves with their dialectic counterpart, the directly religious eighteen edifying discourses which Kierkegaard wrote and published in his own name. On the other hand, all the works of the third group are exclusively religious with the exception of the small, pseudonymous article, "The Crisis and a Crisis." This was put together with the religious portion as a brief reminder that "from the beginning it was the aesthetic which had to be left, to be renounced."[30] This corresponds very closely to the role played by the small religious piece, Two Edifying Discourses, which hinted early on in the authorship "that the religious was the goal to be reached . . . ."[31] The Postscript on the other hand was the midpoint between the two groups and became the turning point of the authorship, since it posed the fundamental question of the entire production: "What does it mean to become a Christian?"[32]

Thus we see how the duplicity of the authorship is carefully maintained in the account provided in The Point of View. Kierkegaard was convinced that the only possible interpretation of the authorship was that he had been a religious author from the beginning. To conclude that he was originally "an aesthetic author, who somehow in the course of time changed and became a religious author"[33] would be a complete misunderstanding. In his opinion, had this been the case there would have had to be many more years between the aesthetic and the religious portions of the authorship. Rather, he argued, such a transformation had occurred at the very beginning. Thus, there had been a kind of deliberate duplicity in the authorship from the start.

To understand this duplicity simply in terms of, for

example, the opposition between the first and second parts of Either/Or would also be a misunderstanding. In fact, the duplicity is that in the pairing of Either/Or and Two Edifying Discourses at the start of the authorship, and in the juxtaposition of "The Crisis and a Crisis" with the last religious works at its end. "The religious is present from the very beginning. Conversely, the aesthetic is once more present at the very last moment."[34] So there was duplicity from start to finish. This was precisely what Kierkegaard believed and sought to demonstrate.

One might conclude from this account, and indeed from the schema included at the end of this paper, that Kierkegaard had a complete and detailed plan for the entire authorship when he began writing in 1843. This was not the case, and such a conclusion runs against Kierkegaard's own retrospective view. For example, in the journals he says: "Indirect communication has been as if instinctive within me, because in being an author I no doubt have also developed myself, and consequently the whole movement is backwards, which is why from the very first I could not state my plan directly, although I certainly was aware that a lot was fomenting within me."[35]

In the beginning of Two Edifying Discourses Kierkegaard used the formula which he would later repeat almost ritualistically: ". . . that individual whom with joy and gratitude I call my reader."[36] He also came to refer to the "single individual" in every volume of these discourses. In these ways he sought to emphasize the "single individual" as the essential religious category. Once again it is possible to see here how the authorship was religious from the beginning. In other words, the movement of the authorship was from the category of the crowd or public to that of the "single individual." As he put it, the authorship eventually attained simplicity.[37]

Kierkegaard had only one aim in the authorship and that was religious. It is important to note that for him the religious had to be approached by careful reflection. Afterwards, however, there was a movement out of reflection back to the utter simplicity of the religious. This movement, which in retrospect Kierkegaard saw as his own, was a Christian movement; it was the process of becoming a Christian. From a Christian perspective one begins, at least if one is a Kierkegaard, as a poet or philosopher, as a perceptive, analytic person, and only later does one become more and more simple in one's understanding and practice of Christianity. As Kierkegaard himself put it: "One does not come to Christianity by reflection. One actually extracts oneself from everything else by reflection and thus becomes more and more simple—a Christian."[38]

Kierkegaard believed that one lives prospectively but understands retrospectively, by constantly looking backwards. He ventured forth into life to experience and experiment with all sorts and conditions of existence. At the same time he sought to re-experience and understand all of this through retrospective reflection. Thus when he began to write about human existence he was able to use the results of his reflection.

Kierkegaard's understanding of his authorship was marked by the same approach and conviction. Of course he already had the main outlines of what he hoped to accomplish in his writings and little by little he gathered the necessary materials from the Bible and history. He put his own creative abilities to work on these materials but throughout the entire process understood himself as a tool in God's hands. He came to realize this even more clearly as he re-experienced his authorship retrospectively through reflection. He saw that he had been "religiously rigorous," that his life and work had been an expression of the "most rigorous kind of religiousness." As he put it in the journals: "It would be dangerous for a man to know that God is using him; that is why he comes to know it only retrospectively."[39]

There are consequences for the reader in all of this which Kierkegaard expresses thus: "The one who is turned forward, who speaks in loud tones about what he wants to do in the future . . . this sort of person is not in a rigorous sense religious. No, backwards, retrospectively: To live every moment as though there were scarcely no more than a day, or even an hour left in one's life; to live in this manner is to live religiously. But this too can be understood only retrospectively."[40]

Let me conclude by summing up my presentation of the retrospective understanding of Kierkegaard's overall production. Kierkegaard's work can only be understood by beginning at the author's conclusion, working backwards through it, with the writings about the authorship and the journals as parallel sources. And these too have to be read and understood retrospectively.

The retrospective method has the following consequences for the study of Kierkegaard's work. The first pseudonymous writings can be understood only in close dialectical relationship with the edifying discourses written at the same time. Moreover the whole of the first part of the authorship before 1846 can be understood only against the background of its repetition on a qualitatively higher level in the later specifically Christian writings up to 1851. And these writings can be understood only in terms of their existential consequences, namely, the books and articles containing Kierkegaard's attack on the church. Finally, the overall literary production can be understood only in so far as one employs its expressly retrospective parts as sources.

The practice of retrospective understanding which I have proposed here also has consequences for particular items in the authorship. For example, what Kierkegaard calls the aesthetic stage or sphere can be understood better from the perspective of the aesthetic-religious stage than in isolation. Similarly, one can better understand the earlier ethical stage in terms of the later religious one towards which it points and to which it is related. But both of these stages are best understood retrospectively, that is, from the rigorously Christian point of view which is the final or ultimate one in Kierkegaard's entire authorship. The point is that Kierkegaard's stages of existence are finally understandable only in terms of the goal to which they lead and from which they are described, namely, the specifically Christian, the mark of which is the striving to imitate Christ.

All of this brings us back to the point at which we began: Kierkegaard's insistence that existence must be lived forwards but can only be understood backwards, after one has lived through it. It is impossible to understand existence before hand. As Climacus says when asserting the impossibility of an existential "system" in the <u>Postscript</u>: "All understanding is afterwards."[41]

In the journals we can follow Kierkegaard's own struggles with existence before he was able to understand it thoroughly and to write about it in the authorship. We can also see how he eventually gained an understanding of the authorship after he had written it. As I have tried to show, this can be read in the journals and particularly in that part of them best known under the title <u>The Point of View for My Work as an Author</u>.

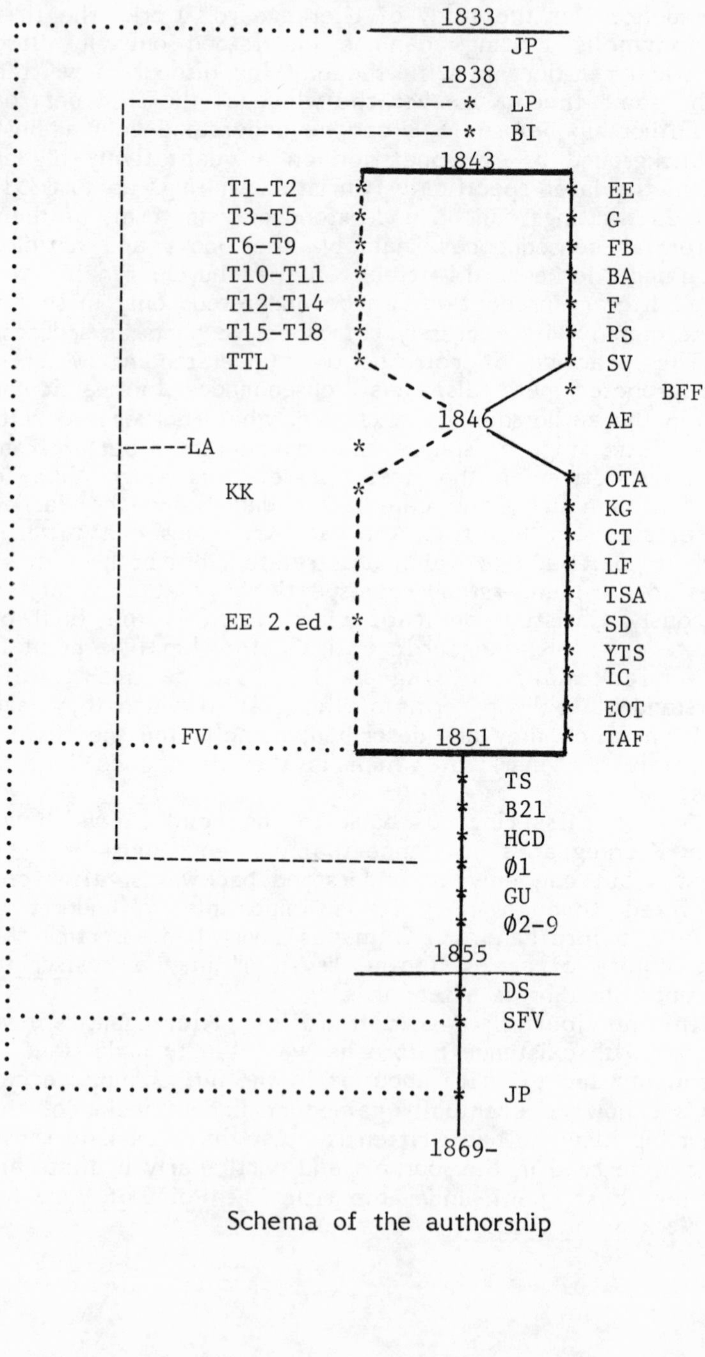

Schema of the authorship

5

TANKE-EXPERIMENT IN KIERKEGAARD

Howard V. Hong

Stephen Leacock or Mark Twain was once asked, "What do you charge for a speaking engagement?" He wrote back saying, "One hundred dollars if I choose the subject and five hundred if you choose a subject——in either case the speech will be the same." Likewise, no matter what the title is on the program, I will present what I have in mind. If I take the title as it stands, I can simply say that in translation Tanke-Experiment in Philosophical Fragments does not come off too badly as "thought-experiment." Now I am done. But I do want to go behind this expression, and therefore I will say much less and also much more than the title promises.

There are those who claim that some terms cannot be translated, or at least should not be translated. If they are translated, it is claimed, there is something misleading; some words should be left just as they are. There are those who extend this position and say that nothing can be translated adequately. Such strictures are admissible if they point primarily to the limitations of translations and to pitfalls in translating, but not if they culminate in the position that every expression is altogether unique and that every language is a completely isolated island. With such stipulations, a translator or linguistic bridge-builder proceeds with Luther's dictum in mind and sins with bold confidence, acknowledging limitations in the ever-present awareness of particular traps.

The first trap for consideration is broad and encompassing, an ectoplasmic trap: syntax. This is the most dangerous trap in translation, because one may deal fairly accurately with words and phrases and ideas but still sin against the second great commandment for translation: thou shalt translate felicitously, thou shalt render ideas in the second language without interloping reminiscences of the first. This trap is vague and ubiquitous, because syntax is the shape of sentences, the connection of terms and phrases, balancing and imbalancing, periodicity, etc. This is not a question of the meaning of terms, the world of the dictionary. It is also more than a matter of conversational fluency and reading ease in a language. A person may have been in a foreign country for a considerable time and have become an expert in that language. But there is such a thing as going native linguistically, so that such a person's translation into his native tongue would be impaired. The translation might have the shape, too much of the shape, of the sentences of his adopted language. It is possible to work for a long time with the texts of a foreign writer, with Kierkegaard, for example, and to go native, so that one's English translations would have a Danish shape. This is a larger trap than the idiom trap of the lady at the embassy in Copenhagen who said she knew it was time to go home because she found herself saying, "Have it good." If the idiom trap is like a sand trap near a golf green, the syntax trap is like an entire golf course of sand.

In our particular work with Kierkegaard's writings, I am the one who could easily go native in translating, simply because I have been reading Kierkegaard in Danish for such a long time. This is where Edna Hong has a very special task. Kierkegaard made a distinction between his writings offered with the left hand and those offered with his right.[1] Edna Hong works on Kierkegaard texts with her left hand and does her own writing with her right hand; therefore she is perhaps the best Danish syntax smasher in the state of Minnesota. This is an achievement. One simply must smash the sentences. If one is attracted too closely to the original shape—— has gone half-native—— then one is seduced linguistically. Here I am saved by having an accomplice.

Terms can also be traps. The first commandment in translating is: thou shalt be faithful to the original. One aspect of this demand for faithfulness is accuracy. It is, of course, possible and sometimes easy to make mistakes, just plain, flat-footed mistakes, in translating. A simple illustration of plain accuracy/inaccuracy in translation is in Journals and Papers (5, 5678; Pap. IV A 132). This version also includes the contribution that sometimes can be made by a compositor along the lines mentioned in the Diapsalmata in Either/Or.[2] The journal entry lists some of the things that might be included in something Kierkegaard intended to write under the title "Pages from the Notebook of a Street Commissioner." As the commissioner walks down the street, he notices a gutter plank out of place. When he reaches the canal where the fishwives sit and sell, he watches them for a while and then contemplates "Torsk og Rødspætter i et Hyttefad." Well, this is not too hard to translate: "cod and flounder in a tank." After volume V of Journals and Papers was published, a reader wrote to us asking that this particular translation be checked. "It sounds all right as it is," he wrote, "but I am curious." Upon checking, I found that with the aid of the compositor, who had changed part of the line in the proofs while correcting another part, the entry reads: "immersed in the contemplation of God and flounder in a tank." And the word was capitalized! Even the coherence test would not bring one up short there, because a Kierkegaardian street commissioner might very well contemplate God and flounder at the same time. It reads all right. This kind of thing can happen, and the final reader may not catch the inaccuracy, because the line does make some sense.

Another aspect of faithfulness is adequacy. This is not quite the same thing as plain accuracy. One can be accurate and can argue for a translation as accurate by pointing to the dictionary, to current usage, to older usage, and so on, but the issue is not thereby settled. Consider the translation of the word Guden in Philosophical Fragments. In a German version some years ago, Christoph Schrempf translated the term as Gott, whereupon Emanuel Hirsch trampled on him, saying that such a translation of Guden is a mark of stiff-necked stupidity.[3] What should be done with a word like that? It is not a common Danish form. It is also uncommon in Kierkegaard. One must go to the context, and the context in Fragments is Plato, who in some places uses the term "the god" (ὁ θεός). A reader of Fragments is supposed to realize that it is a Platonic term; therefore it is not too bad if it comes off as a rather odd expression, "the god." At least it should not be domesticated as a

Hebraic and Christian term, and that was Hirsch's complaint.

Consider also the term Salighed which many have been wrestling with for a long time and which some of you had a chance to hear about in the Canadian Philosophical Association meeting yesterday morning. This term appears, for example, in the epigraph in Fragments. What does history or an historical event have to do with an eternal Salighed? How should it be translated? "Happiness" is accurate, but here in English it is a bit thin, is it not? "Eternal happiness," "bliss," "blessedness," "salvation"? All of these are in a sense accurate, but is any one of them adequate? In the translation of Fragments, we had "salvation" in early versions and rereadings, and we finally turned to "eternal happiness." Why? Again because of the context, again because of Kierkegaard's reading of Plato (also of Aristotle's Nicomachean Ethics), and in keeping with the Platonic character of this hypothetical work or Tanke-Experiment, we turned to "happiness," "eternal happiness," instead of using a more typical Hebraic-Christian term.

The word Virkelighed appears hundreds of times in the Værker and Papirer. In common English usage, we go back and forth perhaps too easily between "actuality" and "reality." We most likely use some form of "real" more than some form of "actual" and make little or no distinction between the two words. But Kierkegaard does not do this. Realitet is used very infrequently in Kierkegaard and except in an early unpublished manuscript is not used more or less synonymously with Virkelighed. Virkelighed pertains to actuality, the temporal and spatial; whereas Realitet pertains to the genuine, the abiding, the eternal. Actuality is a mode of being (not non-being, as Plato has said), but an ontological distinction is made. Realitet is abiding being. Furthermore, a qualitative distinction is made. When Kierkegaard uses the word Realitet, he sometimes means that something is authentic, genuine——for example, if a marriage has Realitet, it is a genuine marriage. A marriage with Realitet is, of course, an actual marriage, but not all marriages have Realitet. In De omnibus dubitandum est, however, these two terms are particularly vexatious, because Johannes Climacus does not distinguish between Virkelighed and Realitet but between Virkelighed-Realitet and Idealitet (ideality).[4] Croxall is quite right, it seems, in stating in a number of notes that Realitet in De omnibus means the same as Virkelighed.[5] Johannes Climacus does not utilize the distinction found in the other works, because his emphasis is on a distinction between thought and actuality-reality. Furthermore, the work is unfinished. If it had been completed, Johannes Climacus would perhaps have arrived at the distinction between "actuality" and "reality" found in the other works under his name. Given the text of De omnibus as it stands, the terms are best translated in a way consistent with translations of the terms in other texts, with the addition of a note or two.

The greatest trap under the rubric of faithfulness is that of familiarity. One thinks one knows, and to be ignorant of one's ignorance is the worst ignorance, because one thinks that one is not ignorant. One readily assumes that one knows. Some simple illustrations. Take the line: "Død, hvor er din Brod?" In a translation of a Norwegian novel, this came out as: "O death, where is thy bread?" Literary familiarity should have protected the translator from the inaccuracy arising from the visual similarity of the familiar word Brød and the quite different word Brod. In a translation of Frygt og Bæven, the words Agnete og Havmanden came off as "Agnes and the half-man" instead of "Agnes and the merman." Many English translators, and we ourselves at times, have confused Christendommen and Christenhed. The misleading similarity of the Danish words and the English words is supplemented by an irregular use of the Danish suffix -hed, so that in translation Christendommen easily becomes "Christendom" and Christenhed becomes "Christianity." This can happen very easily, because the meanings seem obvious on the basis of the translator's familiar mother tongue. Or take an example in Two Ages: "Hvad er det at raisonere?" The English, Germanic, and Romance roots lead English-speaking readers to a readily assumed understanding of familiar looking French terms such as raison in raison d'être. Therefore, "Hvad er det at raisonere?"[6] quite obviously seems to mean "What is it to reason?" It is right there in front of one's nose, and we did translate it that way for a time. But the entire paragraph does not clearly develop the opening thematic sentence. Furthermore, perusal of the Papirer reveals that the word snakke also is used and that it is synonymous with raisonere.[7] In Ludwig Meyer's Fremmedordbog, of which Kierkegaard had two editions,[8] one finds that at raisonere means, among other things, at bruge Mund, "to run at the mouth," "to be loquacious." If the opening line of this particular paragraph is translated "What is reasoning?" or "What is it to reason?" the paragraph does not cohere with its leading sentence. No wonder it is sometimes cited as documentation for and an instance of Kierkegaard's alleged irrationalism or anti-thought. The drafts, however, and the coherence of the paragraph itself both centre on loquacity without essential thought. A Raissoneur is one who pretends to think but is essentially a word-monger. With the translation in terms of loquacity, the paragraph is coherent in itself and also with later portions of Two Ages where the discussion is about what it is to write. An authentic writer is not one who is loquacious about his experiences and personal life; just as in some places there are guards at the door, one guards against evacuating one's personal experiences. The philosophy of art presented here is that writing, apart from memoirs, is a transmutation of any experiential actualities into the realities of the universal. Now the portions of Two Ages hang together: a critique of a specious kind of reasoning, of a dubious kind of reflection, and of a mediocre kind of writing that in loquacity ignore the distinctions between subjectivity and objectivity, silence and speaking. But if the trap of verbal familiarity is not avoided, whole paragraphs and pages are askew because of one word.

An entrapping familiar term of special significance in Kierkegaard's authorship is Experiment in its various forms as a substantive, as a verb, and as participle, present and past. An instance of particular interest and importance is the subtitle of Repetition in the various drafts.[9] At first the subtitle was "A Fruitless Venture [Forsøg]," then "A Venture of Discovery," and again "A Fruitless Venture." Forsøg is and was the most common Danish term close to the English "experiment." Then the subtitle was changed to "A Venture [Forsøg] in Experimental- [Experimental] Philosophy," which was then changed to "Venture in the Experimenting [den experimenterende] Philosophy," and finally "Philosophy" was changed to "Psychology." "Psychology" is itself a term that traps and misleads because of obvious familiarity, but consideration of it will be omitted here, except to say that "experimental psychology" would be almost universally understood in the Anglo-American world in a way altogether inappropriate to Kierkegaard's thought.

In Danish, the word Experiment (in its various forms)

is a loan word.[10] In Kierkegaard's time, the common Danish expression was Forsøg (test, trial, venture), or gøre Erfaring (literally, "to make experience"), or Undersøgelse (investigation), rather than Experiment or the verb experimentere. Neither Danske Orbog, I-VIII (Copenhagen: 1793-1905; ASKB A II 5-8) nor Molbech's Dansk Ordbog (Copenhagen: 1833; ASKB 1032) includes Experiment in any form.

Although the term Experiment was not unknown in Danish of the time, it was not commonly used, and the form used in the subtitle was even more unusual: the present participle, experimenterende. The deleted adjectival form, experimental, has not been located anywhere else either in Kierkegaard's works or in the Papirer.[11] The active character of the participle is still more pronounced in Frater Taciturnus's later use of "experiment" as a transitive verb when he says he will "experimentere en Figur."[12] Although a twentieth-century English-speaking reader of Danish as well as most Danish readers would now customarily read Experiment as "experiment" and experimentere as the verb "experiment," one cannot read "experiment a character" without adding—erroneously—"with" or "on," which are not needed if Kierkegaard's uncommon understanding and use of the transitive verb are used to define it.

Fortunately, Kierkegaard's notes on his reading, recorded in his journals and papers, and also certain of his works make his meaning clear. In the autumn of 1837, while reading Johann Erdmann's Vorlesungen über Glauben und Wissen (Berlin: 1837; ASKB 479), Kierkegaard made note of Erdmann's stress on the role of hypothesis or theory in relation to experiment: "reason experiments [imaginatively reconstructs] when it terminates in making experiences."[13] The universal, the law, the hypothesis is a rational abstraction from experience, and then the hypothesis must find confirmation through the experiment, which first of all is an imaginary construction cast in an experiential mode as a guide for "making experience"; yet the hypothesis is superior and in a sense independent. Reason uses the particularity of the experiment or imaginary experiential construction for the sake of the hypothesis, the universal. Erdmann's epistemology is essentially Aristotelian, with more emphasis on the return to experience than is usually attributed to Aristotle.

A journal entry[14] some months later (5 February 1839)

states that poetry transfigures life by explaining, illuminating, and developing it, an idea reinforced later by Kierkegaard's reading of Aristotle in connection with a contemplated series of lectures on aesthetics to be opened with a lecture on the concept of poetry.[15] "'All poetry is imitation' (Aristotle)——'better or worse than we are.' Hence poetry points beyond itself to actuality and to the metaphysical ideality."[16] Note is taken elsewhere of Aristotle's distinction between ποιεῖν and πράττειν (to make and to act) and his definition of art (in Nicomachean Ethics) as a making.[17] The poet is, then, as the word states, a maker——a maker in the realm of the possible rather than in the realm of what is or has been.[18] Although there is no extant journal reference to Aristotle's dictum that poetry is truer or more philosophical than history, Kierkegaard could hardly have missed it in his reading about poetry as imitation, an observation that does appear explicitly two years later in Stages.

In a journal entry from 1842, Kierkegaard quotes from Lessing.[19] In a later retrospective entry, he writes: "Lessing's whole book 'On the Fable' must be read again. . . . It is found in Sämtl. Werke, vol. XVIII. On pages 204, 205, especially, there is something about Aristotle's teaching about actuality and possibility, and Lessing's teaching concerning it. It agrees so perfectly with what I have developed through several pseudonyms; therefore I have preferred Experimentet to the historical-actual."[20] Although the term Experiment has not yet been found in Lessing's volume XVIII or elsewhere, Johannes Climacus in a draft[21] (1845) and also in the published text of Postscript refers to Lessing and the inverted relationship of one who, "experimenterende [present participle, active], raises doubts without explaining why he does it, and of one [Climacus] who, experimenterende, seeks to show forth the religious in its preternatural magnitude without explaining why he does it."[22]

Numerous entries in the journals and papers indicate what Kierkegaard means by Experiment and experimenterende and how these terms crystallize an epistemology and a philosophy of art involving Aristotle, Plato, and Lessing—— and Kierkegaard, who at the last minute added the word to the subtitle of Repetition.[23]

The task of the poet includes the philosophic one of casting private and shared experience into reflection, of penetrating it and grasping its internal coherence and meaning, the universally human. History and actuality are thereby transcended, and thus poetry, as well as all art, science, and philosophy, deals only with possibility, "not in the sense of an idle hypothesis but possibility in the sense of ideal actuality."[24] Therefore, the poet is "one who makes," who construes, constructs, and composes hypotheses as do the philosophers and the scientists. What distinguishes the poet is a kind of imagination that shapes the possibles in palpable form, in the form of "ideal actuality." The poet's mode is not the discursive, demonstrative, didactic [docerende] mode of the scientist and philosopher or the strict narrative mode of the historian. His mode is that of imaginative construction in the artistic illusion of actuality, or, to borrow a phrase from Climacus in Fragments, it is to construct imaginatively or to hypothesize "in concreto"[25] rather than to use the scientific and philosophic mode of abstraction in his presentation.

The poet in this view is an imaginative constructor [Experimentator] who presents the possible in experiential verisimilitude, and for the existential philosopher "the portrayal of the existential is chiefly either realization in life or poetic presentation, loquere ut videam [speak that I may see]."[26] Kierkegaard is therefore the poetic Experimentator who makes or fashions the various pseudonymous, poetic, imaginative constructors who in turn imaginatively shape characters, scenes, situations, and relations expressive in various ways of the hypothesis(es) in-forming the work. Experimentere is therefore a transitive verb: imaginatively and reflectively to construct a hypothesis and imaginatively to recast it and its implications in the constructed poetic illusion of experiential actuality. Therefore, the task of Frater Taciturnus in Stages is to "experiment a character," imaginatively to construct a character, not to experiment with or on a character. Likewise, Johannes de Silentio is "a poetic [experimented, imaginatively "made"] person who exists only among poets,"[27] who in turn is the dialectical poet who poetizes or "experiments" ethical-religious issues in the form of ideal actuality in the imaginatively constructed work entitled Fear and Trembling. Accordingly, Åge Henriksen quite justifiably calls the work a novel,[28] a category in which he includes especially "The Seducer's Diary" in Either/Or, Repetition, and "'Guilty?'/'Not Guilty?'" in Stages.[29]

For Kierkegaard, Experiment and experimentere as a verb go back essentially, although not verbally, at least as far as his reading of Schleiermacher's Vertraute Briefe über die Lucinde [Schlegel], which he regarded as

> an example of how such a thing can be most productive, in that he constructs a host of personalities out of the book itself and through them illuminates the work and also illuminates their individuality, so that instead of being faced by the reviewer with various points of view, we get instead many personalities who represent these various points of view. But they are complete beings, so that it is possible to get a glimpse into the individuality of the single individual and through numerous merely relatively true judgments to draw up our own final judgment. This is a true masterpiece.[30]

Here is the seed of Kierkegaard's indirect method, the use of imaginary constructions, "experiments," rather than actual descriptions or formal discursive arguments. Ten years later, in an entry from 1845, he states explicitly:

> Later I again found illumination of the meaning of imaginary construction [Experiment] as the form of communication.
>
> If existence is the essential and truth is inwardness, . . . it is also good that it is said in the right way. But this right way is precisely the art that makes being such an author very difficult . . . . If this is communicated in a direct form, then the point is missed; then the reader is led into misunderstanding . . . .[31]

For Kierkegaard himself, the use of the terms Experiment and experimentere had some fateful personal consequences which arose from two misunderstandings. Before Kierkegaard's "First and Last Declaration" (unnumbered pages at the end of Postscript), in which he acknowledged being the poetic fashioner of the pseudonymous authors, who themselves fashioned the imaginary constructions, the works and characters, the pseudonymous works were attributed to him by rumor and even in print. It was also thought by a growing number that these pseudonymous works——especially "The Seducer's Diary" in Either/Or and "'Guilty?'/'Not Guilty?'" in Stages, as well as Fear and Trembling and Repetition——were nothing other than thinly disguised autobiography, personal history, and not categories poetically-dialectically set in motion in the form of imaginary ideal actuality: ideas made visible. That Regine would interpret the works as addressed by him to her——and that she would think of him as a scoundrel and deceiver—was part of his plan; on the other hand, that the poetic-dialectical productions were taken by some as autobiographical reports was the result of a misconception of the facts and of the works and of the nature of the Experimentator (the poet-philosopher).

The second misunderstanding arose from a scientific conception of "experiment" and from the surmise that particularly "the Seducer" (Either/Or) and Quidam (Stages) in Baconian fashion[32] vexed or tortured their subjects experimentally in the practice of a kind of vivisection. P. L. Møller wrote in Gæa (dated 1846 but actually published in December 1845):

> the transparency in our author [of Stages] seems to be a result of poisoning. And, of course, the feminine nature placed on the experimental rack turns into dialectic in the book and vanishes, but in actual life she inevitably must go mad or into Peblinge Lake. . . .
>
> If ordinary common sense may be permitted to intervene here, it perhaps would say in elemental immediacy: If you regard life as a dissecting laboratory and yourself as a cadaver, then go ahead, lacerate yourself as much as you want to; as long as you do not harm anyone else, the police will not disturb your activity. But to spin another creature into your spider web, dissect it alive or torture the soul out of it drop by drop by means of experimentation, that is not allowed, except with insects, and is there not something horrible and revolting to the healthy human mind even in this idea?[33]

The consequences of the twin misunderstandings of the works as factually autobiographical and of "experiment" as the artful vexation of nature in the natural sciences are summarized by Georg Brandes as follows:

> But the moment Kierkegaard broke his engagement, his first hostile collision with the surrounding world entered into the earnest inner conflict of duties. For the first time, his fine, sensitive nature came into hostile contact with town gossip or what in Copenhagen is commonly called public opinion. It treated him badly. Certain features of unreasonableness or hardness towards his betrothed (which, insofar as they were the case, were all due to his efforts to make the young girl weary of him, to put himself in a bad light before her and thereby ease the break for her) were rumored about the city, and the multitude, who had no clue to these singularities in conduct, attributed them to the worst characteristics: coldness of heart, a tendency to play with a human heart in order, as it was called, to "make experiments" with it, something the bourgeois philistines found all the more terrible the less clear a conception they had of what they

actually meant by it. In brief, the most intimate relationship in his life was thrown on the dissecting table, his private life picked to pieces, his betrothed deplored, dirtied, judged. He suffered under it. Although mere words seem to be able to do little harm, it was hard for him to know that this woman's name, which to him was precious, that this name, which he himself could not even hear without feeling, as he says, an electric shock through his body, to know that it was falling, twisted up in town gossip, from all those prattling, defiling lips in an atmosphere of impure minds. And it was hard for him—who, self-respecting and rigorous towards himself and with much sacrifice, honestly examined every action to determine the possibility of its being carried out without a stain on the shield of honor—it was hard for him to be a witness to the way a whole city emptied out its foul vessels on that shield. It was hard to read in impudent and inquisitive looks the judgment of the mob, hard to hear the silence signifying that at the first opportunity there would be talk about one's innermost affairs.[34]

Regine herself knew that the popular notion of Kierkegaard as an "experimenter" on the human heart—namely, hers—was false. Hanne Mourier, a friend of Regine Schlegel, put portions of some of their conversations into writing, which was then read and approved by Regine. On this point, Hanne Mourier writes:

After your husband's death, interest in the story of your youth, your engagement to S. Kierkegaard, has again come to the fore, and many direct approaches have been made to you about this. At first you felt overwhelmed by this interest and spoke about the matter reluctantly, because for many years you lived a completely private and happy life with your husband, and almost no one has dared to approach you with indiscreet questions. Now it is your duty to communicate what you and no one else can: what view you and your husband have had of S. Kierkegaard. You desire that later generations shall be informed about S. Kierkegaard and your noble husband in relation to you and shall see them in the true and good light in which you have known both of them. It must be said and positively maintained that S. Kierkegaard has never misused your love in order to torment you or to conduct mental experiments with you, as has been commonly but erroneously assumed. When he became engaged, it was his earnest intention to marry you. In these later years, you speak of this relationship with many people with whom you associate, because you desire that it be understood that S. Kierkegaard's life was not in any way at variance with his work as a religious author.[35]

On the Danish side, the misunderstanding of Experiment was the result of an entrapment in a specialized, reductive meaning of a term that Kierkegaard used in its elemental fullness and rootedness. In the English translation, the easy entrapment in the familiar English word is again reductionist and is inadequate to the depth and range of Kierkegaard's use of the term for the poet-philosopher's indirect method. The various and important consequences of both misunderstandings of a single word illustrate the ironic observation in Either/Or: "At times, from enormous and mighty causes, very slight and insignificantly small effects sometimes appear; at times, a nimble little cause gives rise to a colossal effect."[36]

Comment on Hong

Robert L. Perkins

Professor Hong's paper takes us to the very heart of the issues raised in translation. His proposal is that the expression Kierkegaard tried as a subtitle to Repetition is opaque and requires interpretation.

Hong's example is much like the one Eugene Nida used in his great work, Toward a Science of Translation: With Special Reference to Principles and Procedures Involved in Bible Translating.[37] Nida cites as an example St. Paul's expression "Greet one another with a holy kiss." That strange expression makes us realize the great cultural differences separating Paul's time from our own. The kiss was then used as a form of greeting in a much wider circle than we use it today. Now, does one just translate literally and depend on persons to intuit the cultural difference? Or does one translate, improve, and update the expression, "Greet each other with a hearty handshake all around"?

In Hong's particular instance, the question is whether he should more or less literally translate "A Venture in Experimenting Psychology" by "A Venture in Imaginary Psychological Construction"? Der er en lille forskell.

Briefly, Hong's argument is that "experiment" is misleading in English. Therefore, this expression must be replaced by some form of "imaginatively construct." He illustrates this with numerous examples which he hopes will enable us to understand better many opaque passages in Kierkegaard's writings and journals.

Hong then widens his point in a second move in his paper. Taking his lead from the quotation about

Schleiermacher and other journal entries on indirect method he concludes that "experiment" as a noun or as a verb is synonymous with Kierkegaard's method of indirect communication. This is the method of the poet-philosopher who poeticizes or imaginatively constructs the pseudonymous writers who in turn imaginatively construct the numerous characters in the writings as 'experiments'. This is not exactly what the present-day English reader expects when he encounters the expression "experimental psychology." Of course, that expression cannot be used. The question is: How inventive can a translator become?

However, we wonder whether his translation may not be a bit overripe. For instance, why did Kierkegaard use the expression he did rather than the one Hong has imaginatively constructed from his "experimenting psychology?" Was Kierkegaard attempting to be novel and instead became merely obscure? Is the subtitle a mere affectation which requires the imaginative reconstruction offered by Hong? Is it not possible that Kierkegaard said exactly, indeed precisely, what he intended? Has not the interpretation gone beyond the limits permitted a translator?

To press the latter question, can we seriously maintain that "imaginative construction" is an accurate translation of "experimenterende psychologie"? Kierkegaard's words have obvious transliterations into English. Hong's arguments that we must adopt his expression have an initial plausibility, but is it not possible that interpretation-translation has become invention?

Look at the issue this way: Will the English reader of Hong's translation of Kierkegaard's Repetition be in a better position to understand the meaning than the poor Jutlander who must depend on Kierkegaard's original but obscure Danish?

Even if we admit that "imaginatively construct" counts as a translation of "experimenterende," we may still ask what happened to "Psychologie." I do not find it accounted for in Hong's proposed translation. Indeed, his translation appears to invent a new meaning on the one hand and to omit a significant element of the phrase in question on the other. Hong's effort may be a dangerous precedent in translating.

Perhaps the issue can be put most simply this way. Whether in the final publishable draft of Repetition Hong uses Kierkegaard's "experimenting psychology" or his own "imaginative construction," a long, tedious, and argumentative footnote must be written to explain either Hong's imaginative construction or Kierkegaard's own obscure expression. So Hong, as a translator, must choose which translation to publish and which footnote of explanation to write. I am sure many English readers, in keeping with many of the questions I have raised, would urge him to play it safe by keeping to the more literal translation, experimenting psychology, and writing a footnote in which he explains the meaning as "imaginatively construct." I admit that has considerable appeal to me, but it must be rejected.

I believe that the long range interests of interpreting Kierkegaard to the English-speaking world require not only this "imaginative construction" but many more. The reason is one which Hong has intuited: the reader must be given the best interpretation on the printed page of the text. That is as far as many will or need to go. We can put the qualifications, the niceties and the debate in the footnotes. Therefore, in the words of Staupitz to Luther, "Hong, sin bravely." Those of us who have been reading Hong's translations for several years have no doubt that he will continue to do so. We are fortunate that such a sinner combines such gifts of translation and interpretation. If you do not like my calling Hong a sinner, I can rewrite this paragraph using an Italian proverb about traitors and translators.

The second thesis of Hong's paper is that "experimenting psychology" or, as he expresses it, "imaginative construction," is synonymous with the method of indirect communication. On this point he offers numerous passages where his proposed translation-interpretation is used, and to good effect, to illuminate these passages.

However, there are problems with this view. The first is that this thesis which spreads over the whole authorship does not do anything to illuminate Repetition, the very place where the expression shows most vividly. Further, it will require long and tedious explanations each time it is used in Kierkegaard's writings.

The second problem with this view is that it construes Kierkegaard's work as a 'poetry,' the poetry of inwardness. This construal casts Kierkegaard in an unwholesome light so far as recent and ancient philosophy is concerned simply because the relation of poetry and truth claims remains obscure even for non-positivistic philosophers. Those of us who are philosophers find ourselves in a quite unhappy position, for our preferred commitments are to those areas and disciplines in which truth claims can be established. Hong's thesis would emphasize the poetic and the imaginative and serves further to isolate Kierkegaard from philosophy.

To be sure, there are still some passages by Kierkegaard's imaginatively constructed authors which bear on philosophic issues. There are also some well-constructed philosophic arguments. The problem is to separate these few arguments from their context of poetic ideality and to relate them to the cold and brazen world of ordinary truth claims and current conceptions of actuality. Can these arguments hold their own in the unpoetic and uninspired world of philosophic analysis? Hong's paper has helped me to see much more clearly why the vast majority of Anglo-Saxon philosophers have tended to ho-hum Kierkegaard. It has also compelled me to wonder whether I should not either ask for a transfer from the philosophy department to the department of literature where I could more properly continue work on the poetic and imaginative constructions of Kierkegaard or to give up Kierkegaard and turn my attention to less diffuse and poetic efforts and problems in philosophy.

The contest between poetry and philosophy is of course not new. Hong's paper may settle some issues in translation, but it also shows that, like Plato's, Kierkegaard's was a poetically expressed philosophy which aimed to transcend poetry in order to arrive at truth. Such a combination involves both structural and conceptual tension which will require much more than another merely imaginative construction to overcome.

6

COMMUNICATION AND COMMUNITY

Jeremy Walker

I begin by stating a problem in Kierkegaard's thought. I shall state it only briefly, and therefore vaguely. In the rest of my essay I try to display a way by which this problem can be attacked. Again I do so only summarily.

The problem is a problem of understanding. It arises for me because Kierkegaard asserts four propositions which do not evidently belong to a single consistent theory. To solve this problem would be to state such a theory. I do not claim to state the theory in my essay. I do not even claim that it can be stated. We cannot know whether this is possible or not in advance of actually possessing the detailed, rigorous, and complete construction.

In this respect, as in other more important respects, my essay is very far from being a communication of results.

1.

Here are four propositions which Kierkegaard asserts:

1. Becoming a Christian entails becoming an individual.
2. One individual can communicate with another, about the spiritual or inward, only indirectly.
3. A Christian essentially loves his neighbour.
4. Loving one's neighbour entails spiritual communication.

From these four propositions I infer that, according to Kierkegaard, Christian love is a form of indirect, not direct, communication. This is the position which I do not understand. I do not grasp clearly and definitely the concepts which frame Kierkegaard's position. And I cannot see fully and rigorously the deductions which uphold it.

2.

Becoming an individual entails acquiring inwardness. Inwardness is not a state, or even a process. It is more like a capacity for penetrating one's own mind and heart, and a habit of exercising this capacity as continuously as possible. This is why it makes no sense to talk of achieving inwardness. It is in the nature of inwardness to be ever deepening itself. We can distinguish several stages of deepening inwardness.

First, there is the kind of self-knowledge which Plato writes about in his Socratic dialogues, especially in the Apology. This is knowledge which is gained through self-examination, and properly expressed in a certain kind of explanatory account of one's own life. Kierkegaard often uses the words deposition (Forklaring) and testimony (Vidnesbyrd) for such an account. As the paradigm of Socrates shows, a deposition is not autobiographical but ethical. It is not historically or psycho-analytically extensive. It is ethically intensive, and reveals the architectonic ideals and principles which have ruled one's life, and one's life as the continual attempt to obey and express them.

To commit oneself to the Socratic pursuit of self-knowledge is to commit oneself also to a certain general idea of truth. It is to commit oneself to what modern logicians call a 'realist' idea of truth. The idea of self-knowledge as an ethical goal can have no sense, for example, for a pragmatist or a constructivist. It could be given sense by also adopting an anti-realist analysis of ethical assertions. But then one's pursuit of self-knowledge would be wholly un-Socratic.

However, the Socratic project breaks down when the individual reaches a certain depth of inwardness. It is the depth at which one recognises that there are forces in oneself which are essentially hostile to the discovery of deep truths about oneself. To recognise this fact is also to acknowledge the inadequacy of one's former ideas of truth and the self.

We encounter now the second stage of inwardness, which I shall call 'Stoic'. Here the individual adopts an idea of truth as not only objective but absolute and transcendental. This is part of what Kierkegaard means by 'eternal'. At the same time, the individual acknowledges that the self which he seeks to know is also a transcendental being. We encounter here the first application of a principle which is central in Kierkegaard's thought. This is the principle, plainly stated in SD, that the self is identified by that in the face of which the individual consciously identifies his self.

If the Stoic life breaks down, it is again because the individual goes beyond a certain depth of inwardness. If the truth against which I measure myself is eternal, then in comparison the 'I' which is measured against the truth is nothing——an empty vanishing point. As soon as I abandon the objective standpoint of logic or metaphysics, therefore, I shall find myself to be in despair. I shall be in the despair of bondage to a categorical ethical law which I cannot fulfil, and whose fulfilment has no meaning.

If one is to escape from such despair, it can only be by a further deepening of inwardness. This change must take the form, to speak in psychological language, of a more intense passion in the face of the eternal. This more intense passion is consciousness of sin and confession of one's sins.

There cannot be, in Kierkegaard's thought, any logical transition from the Stoic stage to the present stage. Nor can there be a natural psychological transition. Nature merely takes us to the despair of Stoicism and abandons us there. Whatever throws an individual into the deeper inwardness of the confession of sin must be something other than natural reason, desire, or will. It must be an external power. I do not mean a power external to one's body or one's mind. I mean a power which operates from a region within one which is still deeper than the deep self discovered in Stoic inwardness.

God is thus first experienced in the act of confession of sins. To borrow Kierkegaard's acoustical metaphor, one who is confessing at the same time hears an echo of his own confession in which he himself is being addressed as 'Thou'. To hear this echo is to hear God pronouncing judgement on one. It is to find oneself before an Eternity which exists, an Absolute who is a person.

To exist before the face of God, however, is not yet in itself to exist as a Christian. The Christian only exists face to face with Jesus Christ. Such an existence is a still deeper potentiation of inwardness than any stage so far identified.

We are all familiar with Kierkegaard's claim that Christianity is not founded on historical evidence. At the same time he emphasizes that the Christian must first encounter Christ as Jesus, the individual of history. To meet Jesus is to meet an actual man, once living and now dead. That experience is not yet in itself the experience of meeting Christ. To meet Christ one must accept that Jesus was Christ, the incarnate God. This requires an act of faith which has bypassed or overcome the shock of offence naturally caused by that identification.

The individual who accepts Jesus as Christ thereby adopts a quite radically new idea of truth. He adopts the amazing idea that truth is not a logical or epistemological relation, but a way of being; indeed, a person. From now on, Christian philosophy must be founded on the premiss that Jesus Christ is the way and the truth and the life.

At this stage the individual has encountered God as incarnate in Christ. But he has encountered Christ only as the pattern, the teacher. Neither logically nor psychologically is this the last possible stage. The last stage is to encounter Christ as the redeemer. It is to experience Christ as atoning for one's own sins by his death on the Cross. To do this is not, of course, only to accept the doctrine or a particular doctrine of the Atonement. It is to experience another person's making an act of atonement for oneself. We must remember that, according to Kierkegaard, the Christian is not an individual who holds certain beliefs; he is an individual who finds himself to be existing in a situation of contemporaneity with Jesus Christ. An essential element in this situation is that Christ is sacrificing his life out of pure love to bring it about that we are forgiven by God. The experience of God, therefore, is now experience of a God who is loving; indeed, love.

The self which comes to exist and is acknowledged in this experience is one's deepest and true self. The only true self-knowledge is knowledge of oneself as revealed in the light of the Atonement. It follows, according to Kierkegaard's central principle, that the true self is a self whose proper measure is an absolutely self-sacrificial love.

In short, spirit is love.

Thus I end the first part of my summary argument. Before I start the next part, I want to make three remarks. First, I apologise for the vagueness and inexactness of what I have just been saying. I am a theological ignoramus, and intended no precise and specific doctrines by my words. Second, I emphasize the quite central importance for Kierkegaard of the idea of the Atonement. In my view, his thought will be unintelligible as a single consistent theory if that idea is not given its proper central place in his thought. It follows, third, that Kierkegaard's own doctrine of the Atonement must be given a detailed and rigorous analysis. I am quite incompetent to say anything about this. None the less, I am forced to state one opinion. Kierkegaard occasionally speaks of the Atonement in the language of substitution and propitiation, but I do not believe that this language expresses his views fully or adequately. It suggests that God's justice and love are distinct operations, which are related to each other only externally. Kierkegaard did not accept this idea. "What you do unto men you do unto God, and therefore what you do unto men God does unto you."[1] To the individual whose spirit is justice, God is justice; to the individual whose spirit is becoming love, God is love.

3.

To become an individual is to become qualified as spirit. For to be an individual is to have or be a self. To be a self is to exist in a certain kind of way. And existing most deeply in that way is existing as a spirit.

According to Kierkegaard, the idea of a self is the exact logical correlate of the idea of reflection. Reflection is action directed upon its own source. If we take seriously the idea of action, we shall see why in Kierkegaard's thought the idea of reflection is properly used only in the sphere of psychology, and not in the spheres of logic or natural science. The only proper example of reflection is self-consciousness, thinking about oneself. Kierkegaard's idea of the self, therefore, is contextually defined as the subject-object of reflection. There is no viable alternative to a contextual definition. In particular, it is inept to approach this idea of the self with a list of Aristotelian categories in hand, asking, 'Is the self a substance? a property? a relation?', and so on.

However, we require a second essential qualification. According to Kierkegaard, merely thinking about oneself is not necessarily acting upon oneself. The more objective thinking becomes, the less it admits an individual subject. The essential subject of pure thinking is not a particular individual, say René Descartes, but a pure ego. And a pure ego is an epistemological fiction; an hypostasisation of objective knowledge. That is why Kierkegaard remarks that a man who lacks a will is not a self. Reflection, therefore, means not observing oneself but acting on oneself. It is a kind of thinking about oneself which is essentially transformative.

The remark that a man who lacks a will is not a self should alert us to the fact that in Kierkegaard the self is as far as possible from being an abstract contentless entity. The true self is not something we discover only behind or through our empirical characteristics. On the contrary, the idea that my empirical character is not 'the real me' precisely indicates one of the subtlest forms of despair. Certainly Kierkegaard is not a behaviourist, because he denies that the inner must be commensurable with the outer. On the other hand, he is not a transcendental idealist either. The true self is character, since character is inwardness.

Mutatis mutandis, the same holds for Kierkegaard's idea of individuality. Individuality is both the deepest inwardness and the most continuous, consistent concretion.

Anti-Climacus defines the self in its most potentiated form as 'grounded transparently in the Power which posited it.' Transparency is an idea whose literal sense is hard to grasp. In Kierkegaard's thought, it is used to refer to some function of a man's knowledge or vision of himself. The metaphor is seeing an object more or less clearly through a medium which is more or less directly penetrable by light. Yet the distinction between medium and object cannot be made in the case of self-knowledge. Moreover, in this case the object is also identical with the observer. Hence transparency, in Kierkegaard's thought, is primarily a qualification of an activity, the activity of thinking about oneself.

For this reason, we can relate transparency and continuity. Kierkegaard identifies existing as spirit with having essential continuity. Continuity means continuity in self-consciousness. But this is not at all the same as thinking continually and exclusively about oneself. The mark of essential continuity is the ability to give an essentially continuous, consistent account of one's life. Such an account is the confession of one's sins, which are recognised to be particular manifestations of an underlying continuity in sin.

Individuality, like selfhood, implies the idea of a ground. The ground, the source and origin, of all individuality, is God. Individuality is a gift from the Creator. In making these claims, Kierkegaard is denying both that individuality is a product of natural processes and that it is constructed by the individual himself ex nihilo. We cannot create our own individualities at will, because whenever we become aware of ourselves we find ourselves to be essentially concrete. Not only our circumstances but our natural characteristics are given to us as data for the work of making ourselves transparent. At the same time, the task is not so much to see our natural characters clearly as to assume responsibility for them in the light of a consciousness of sin.

It is crucial to Kierkegaard's idea of spirit that there is no natural or direct continuity between the kind of selfhood which precedes all self-reflection and spirit. There is a breach which is marked by dying to the world. It is precisely here that the individual's own powers cease. If one is to acquire spirit in place of natural selfhood, it can only be because spirit is communicated to one. This communication is God's work.

Individuality is therefore, according to Kierkegaard, the final result of God's communicating his spirit to someone who already, presumably, has natural characteristics and a moral will. There is a curious temptation to imagine the communication of spirit as the infusion of some homogeneous characterless substance, so that everything we normally call 'character' will be suppressed or destroyed. This curious idea is strengthened by the temptation to imagine that dying to the world must mean the drying up of the natural springs of passion and action. There are passages where Kierkegaard appears to be saying such things. But any such ideas are quite certainly contrary to the whole thrust of his thinking; besides, they are intrinsically nonsensical.

4.

To become spirit is to acquire spiritual qualities; it is for the particular qualities which characterize one to become spiritual qualities. I take the idea of a spiritual quality to be crucial in my present attempt to elucidate the structure of Kierkegaard's thought.

Kierkegaard talks about spiritual qualities in two cardinal passages. One passage occurs towards the end of the chapter in KG in which he argues for the identity of love and the upbuilding. The other is the third discourse of Part II of CT. Shortly I shall analyse these passages. But I must first consider two more basic issues. Each arises from the idea of appropriation.

Ordinarily, we distinguish between coming to possess a quality and actually possessing it. In Kierkegaard's view, this distinction cannot be made for spiritual qualities. With them, there is no such state as a possessing which is the result of a process of coming to possess that is now finished. Further, coming to possess a spiritual quality cannot just happen to one. Spiritual qualities are appropriated only in freedom. Charity, for example, is not a quality of the kind one can be born with or just happen to acquire while growing up. There are certainly natural facsimiles of true charity. But one can possess true charity only through striving to possess it. And it is nonsense to imagine that there exists a point where one may cease to strive because one now finally possesses charity. Charity can be exercised only in acts each one of which, through one's entire life, must be wholly original.

Let us now look at the two passages from KG and CT.

> The qualities a man can possess must be either qualities he has for himself, even if he makes use of them in relationship to others, or qualities for others. Wisdom is a characteristic for oneself; power, talents, knowledge, and such are likewise qualities for oneself. To be wise does not mean to presuppose that others are wise . . . . Because wise is an exclusive characteristic, it is not impossible to suppose that there could be or could have been a wise man who dared say that he assumed all others to be ignorant. In theory . . . there is no contradiction . . . . If, however, one were to think that he loves, but also that all others were unloving, we would say: no, stop; here is a contradiction in pure theory, for to be loving means precisely to assume, to presuppose, that other men are loving. Love is not an exclusive characteristic, but it is a characteristic by which or in virtue of which you exist for others.[2]

. . . . . .

> All earthly and worldly goods are in themselves selfish, invidious, the possession of them, being invidious or envious, must of necessity make others poorer: . . . . Even though a man may be willing to communicate in his earthly goods—yet every instant when he is employed in acquiring them or is dwelling upon the possession of them he is selfish, . . .
>
> It is otherwise with the goods of the spirit. The goods of the spirit are, according to the very concept, communication; the possession of them is merciful, in and for itself it is communication . . . .
>
> . . . . He who strives after or possesses these goods does not therefore do good to himself merely, but bestows a benefaction upon all, labours for all, his effort to acquire these goods does in and for itself enrich others immediately; . . .
>
> . . . . If any man would possess them selfishly, possess them as his own in a selfish sense, he does not possess them at all.[3]

I shall now try to explain briefly what Kierkegaard means in these passages. I do so under two assumptions. First, I assume that Kierkegaard is stating conceptual truths. He is talking, for example, not about particular cases of charitable action but about the idea, the concept, of charity. Second, I assume that the various distinguishable points which Kierkegaard makes about spiritual qualities are neither random nor independent, but are themselves conceptually related to each other. Love is a 'quality for others', not for oneself; and it is a 'quality through which one exists for others', not an 'exclusive quality'. How are these ideas related?

By 'existing for others' Kierkegaard plainly does not mean just 'existing as an object for others' experience.' Trees and stones exist in this manner. Nor, plainly, does he mean just 'existing as a subject for the experience of others.' All of us except real solipsists exist so. Nor does he even mean just 'existing in a way which essentially affects others.' This describes a tyrant or a sadist as well as a saint. So I infer that Kierkegaard means by 'existing for others' existing in a way which is essentially for the good of others.

A wise man, a Socrates, may use his wisdom for the good of others. If so, it is not simply because he is wise. It is because he is concerned about the good of others. But his concern about the good of others is not part of what we mean when we call him 'wise'; and it is not a necessary consequence of his wisdom either. So his existing for others is quite independent of his wisdom. Love, on the contrary, is essentially concern for the good of others. The fact that a loving person acts for the good of others is part of what we mean when we call that person 'loving'. So existing for others is part of love.

Kierkegaard claims, also, that to be loving is to presuppose that love exists in all others. Now how is this latter claim related to the ideas just explicated above?

Let me begin by rephrasing this latter claim. To love is to assume that all others are good; that is, essentially and potentially good. A conceptual relation can now be established. It is because the loving person assumes that others are potentially good that he is concerned to try to build up good in them. And it is because he assumes that they are potentially good that his loving actions often do succeed in building up good in them. Often, a loving action elicits a loving response.

Let us invert this argument. Suppose a person who does not assume that others are essentially loving beings. It would apparently be senseless for this person to act in a way intended to build up love in others. He might reply: "No, for by my loving actions I may be able to create love where none existed before." But this will not do. Either he is asserting an ability to create ex nihilo a capacity for love in others, and this is the assertion of a megalomaniac, or he is implicitly granting that others already have a latent capacity for loving, which his acts merely release; in which case he is granting Kierkegaard's point.

We must be careful not to misconstrue Kierkegaard's claim that spiritual goods are essentially communication. It is plain enough in general what this means. It is in the nature of love to try to act lovingly oneself and to elicit love in others. But we must not picture eliciting love as kindling love, as holding one flame to paper brings another flame into being. In Kierkegaard's view, the love that is latent within each one of us is a direct creation and gift of God.

In fact, the love that is latent within a person is the spiritual individuality which that person has from, and before, God.

But Kierkegaard's idea of spiritual qualities applies not only to love, but also, at least, to faith and hope——the other two cardinal theological virtues. Now how do his ideas fit faith and hope?

We cannot say that it is part of what 'faith' and 'hope'

mean that a person who has faith or hope is essentially concerned to try to bring about the good of others. The connection here is indirect. It can be established as follows. What is it to possess faith and hope, that is the virtues of Christian faith and hope? It is, at least, to believe in a God who is essentially forgiving and loving. But this means believing in a God who forgives and loves all individuals equally. In Kierkegaard's view, nothing could less represent the spirit of Christianity than any idea that forgiveness and love are awarded exclusively, or discriminatorily, or following some kind of comparison between individuals. Even human charity towards one's neighbour cannot admit less than the most rigorous spiritual egalitarianism. So the claim to believe in a God whose gifts are not for all of us without distinction is either not Christian or self-contradictory. If so, it must be a direct consequence of true faith and hope that their possessor wishes to communicate a message of the existence of a forgiving and loving God to all other individuals. For he must wish that they too shall acquire themselves the spiritual goods which are faith and hope. Once again, therefore, although this time indirectly, we reach a like conclusion. To have faith and hope is necessarily to try to communicate faith and hope to others. And, once again, this effort can be carried on only under the assumption that all other individuals are already in essential possession of the pre-requisites for faith and hope.

Thus I end the second part of my summary exposition and argument. Before I continue, I want to make an apologetic aside. I have scarcely even attempted the beginning of a serious analysis of Kierekaard's idea of individuality. Without such an analysis, of course, we cannot seriously claim to grasp Kierkegaard's thought. More generally, I think that there are issues in this area as yet unsuspected by the many philosophers, past and present, who are engaged in discussing personal identity. Whatever 'personal identity' means, it is something more mysterious, positive, and rich than the standard analytical discussions suggest. As one of my colleagues once remarked to me, actual experience with human beings tends to make one want to say that individuals are <u>absolutely</u> distinct; much less like different members of one species than like individual members of quite different species.

5.

The possession of qualities of spirit is in and for itself communication. To exist as spirit is therefore in and for itself to communicate. But to communicate what, and how?

Love is essentially concern to try to bring about the good of others. But what is the good of others? It is precisely their own spiritual good. An individual's spiritual good is his possession of spiritual goods; of spiritual qualities. So his true good is his possession of faith, hope, and charity. Therefore to love is to be concerned that others should come to possess faith, hope, and charity. "Indeed, what is the highest good and the greatest blessedness? Certainly it is to love in truth."[4] And this, let me recall, is the same as existing before Christ the Redeemer.

To love someone is, then, to try to help that person to love God. To be truly loved is to be helped by someone towards the love of God. But how far is this within the actual capacities of any of us? Plainly not far, since loving God, like having faith or hope, is not an accomplishment that any individual can implant in another. To acknowledge this fact is central to love. So the communication of love is a very peculiar kind of communication. It is the effort by one individual to enable another to establish his own relationship with God, where the latter cannot be essentially helped, but can be hindered, by the former, in establishing his own God-relationship. It is in this sense that we should take Kierkegaard's repeated insistence that love is essentially sacrifice. The true lover "is completely and wholly transformed into being simply an active power in the hands of God."[5]

In Kierkegaard's thought, there is a necessary connection between the ideas of love and truth. It is the existence of this necessary connection that defines the Christian understanding of love. To love truly is just to try to communicate the truth. It is: "in love to the truth and to men to will to bring every sacrifice in order to proclaim the truth and nevertheless not to be willing to sacrifice the least bit of the truth."[6] Love, therefore, entails witnessing to the truth.

I do not want to discuss this important Kierkegaardian idea in any detail. Still, I must say a little about it here.

It is a familiar theme in Kierkegaard's pseudonymous works that the inward can be communicated, if at all, only indirectly. But this idea occurs also in some of his Christian works. We may not then ignore the idea in an analysis of Kierkegaard's own thought on the grounds that it is essentially a pre-Christian idea. According to Kierkegaard himself, spiritual truths can be communicated only indirectly.

It appears to follow from this thesis that spiritual relationships between one individual and others cannot go beyond the maieutic. For the maieutic is the essential form of a relationship in which communication is indirect. If so, it must follow that the relationship of true love must also, according to Kierkegaard, be essentially maieutic.

Now it is undoubtedly true that the figure of Socrates, and the Socratic understanding of the individual, remained central to Kierkegaard's Christian thought even in its latest stages. This is plain from SD, TS, and Ø, as well as from SFV and FV. I cite here also a passage from KG which appears to express the same Socratic understanding.

> You have to do only with what you do unto others or with the way you receive what others do unto you; the direction is inwards; essentially you have only to do with yourself before God . . . . In this world of inwardness the Christian like-for-like is at home. It wants to turn you away from the external (but without taking you out of the the world), upwards or inwards. For, Christianly understood, to love human beings is to love God and to love God is to love human beings; what you do unto men you do unto God, and therefore what you do unto men God does unto you.[7]

On the other hand, in these works Socrates does not figure as a pattern of the Christian existence. His significance for the Christian is not positive, like the significance of Abraham or Job. It can be only negative. Christianly understood, the figure of Socrates acts as a corrective to false ideas.

Kierkegaard, in fact, explicitly distinguishes the Christian form of communication from the maieutic. I cite two representative passages. In KG he remarks that Socrates had rightly seen that the highest that one individual can do for another is to make him free.[8] He adds that Socrates' understanding that this requires deliberate self-concealment is shared also by the Christian.

Yet there is a difference of views deeper down. For

Socrates self-concealment is required because the communicator might otherwise mask the appearance of the truth to the other person. For a Christian, it is because he might find himself masking the appearance of God to the other; that is, find himself standing in the way of the other's attempt to establish a solitary relationship with God.

Further, this understanding is accompanied in the Christian by something that Socrates entirely lacked. It is 'a fear and trembling.' The Christian, unlike Socrates, "has understood the danger and the suffering in the midst of the task and above all the terribleness of responsibility." That is to say, the Christian has a loving concern for the true good of the individual he is trying to help. Socrates did not, and could not. For he did not know what true good and evil were. There is a simpler, though cruder, way of making this point. For a Christian, becoming conscious of one's continuity in sin is an essential part of becoming conscious of the truth. So communicating the truth must entail somehow communicating to the other a consciousness of his or her continuity in sin; helping him or her to appropriate this consciousness. So Christian communication has a suffering intrinsic to it which is entirely foreign to the Socratic.

Here is the second representative passage. In his Journals, Kierkegaard writes: "Yet the communication of the essentially Christian must end finally in 'witnessing'. The maieutic cannot be the final form, because, Christianly understood, the truth does not lie in the subject (as Socrates understood it), but in a revelation which must be proclaimed . . . . Ultimately the user of the maieutic will be able to bear the responsibility, for the maieutic approach still remains rooted in human sagacity, however sanctified and dedicated in fear and trembling this may be. God becomes too powerful for the maieutic practitioner and then he is a witness . . . ."[9]

Kierkegaard's crucial thesis, I believe, is that the Christian form of communication, although not maieutic, lies beyond and not on this side of the maieutic. So witnessing to the truth is even farther from being direct communication than is Socratic maieusis. It follows that the relationship of Christian love puts more distance between individuals, not less, than does the Socratic relationship. If it is misleading to say that charity is a form of indirect communication, this is because it states the point not too strongly but too weakly. In Kierkegaard's view, Christianity reveals the existence of a much profounder separation between individuals than any pagan philosopher has imagined. I said above that love 'puts' distance between individuals and I was not using the word loosely. What is the essential work of the witness to the truth? It is "to disintegrate the crowd," to detach the individual from the crowd.[10] What is the essential work of love? It is to help the other towards owning his own soul, "to become one's self, free, independent, his own, help him to stand on his own."[11]

6.

Ever since I first began to discern the problem which I have been trying to address in this essay, I have imagined that to answer the problem completely would require elucidating Kierkegaard's idea of a Christian community, his idea of how Christians should live together. But in the writing of this essay I have come to believe that my understanding was mistaken. I now believe that Kierkegaard had no idea of a Christian community. He had no pattern of a social and political existence to recommend. It is not only that no such pattern can be seen in, or inferred from, a book like KG. A proper understanding of Kierkegaard's position, I now believe, shows that it could not possibly yield any social or political recommendations.

Kierkegaard thought constantly about 'the crowd' and 'the individual'. There is no third concept within his writings which might identify the way in which individuals can exist together in this world. Nor in the other world either.

Comment on Walker

R. H. Archer

There is much in Professor Walker's paper that deserves attention, but I must limit my comments to two matters.

First there is the question of just how the problem arises from the four Kierkegaardian statements which Walker cites at the beginning. The notion of entailment used in them is existential more than logical, and if the third statement is equivalent to "Being a Christian entails loving your neighbour" then the first, third and fourth statements can be seen to be mutually compatible entailments of Christianity in that sense. The problem, then, seems to lie in the second statement, which predicts failure: the communication about love which the individual can manage will not be direct.

Now, this does not seem a serious failure. Indirect communication surely counts as genuine communication in the sense required in the other three statements. There, the entailments are not stated in absolute terms; there is stated only the necessity to become an individual who communicates love to his neighbour. Only if individuality were tantamount to absolute isolation would there be no communication, and the language of indirect communication does not imply that. So it is not clear that the problem of communication is all that severe.

But let us suppose that indirect communication were held to be absolutely inadequate in view of the enormous obligation to witness effectively concerning the eternal. Still, the third statement seems to allow for proper, loving, individual communication, for it says that the indirectness is in the communication about love, not in the communication of love. The difference is crucial and compatible with Kierkegaard's well known rejection of the intellectual as a sufficient means for approaching the infinite. But if we are to love, and the inadequacy is merely in talk about love, the problem evaporates.

For my second comment I turn to the point, among many interesting points, which happens to intrigue me most and which offers an opportunity to move quickly to Walker's conclusion. This is in his treatment of Kierkegaard's statement from Works of Love, "For to be loving means precisely to assume, to presuppose, that other men are loving." Ordinarily this would be judged a falsehood. The term 'to love' does not imply reciprocity. On the contrary, it might be thought a virtue to persevere in love in the face of unloving antipathy. The fact that there is a tendency for love to flag when it is not reciprocated is just that—a fact, and therefore a contingency, not a necessity. I sympathize with Walker's move to accommodate this difficulty by speaking of the necessity in terms of the recognition of a potential to be loving on the part of the other person. But I am uncomfortable with the reduction of the Kierkegaardian claim to a doctrine of mere potential. The statement of it is so clear, so odd, and so strong all at once, that it demands to have its full force preserved if at all possible. I would like to suggest two possibilities.

First, it seems certain that Kierkegaard meant to affirm less about our intellectual or conceptual state than about our existential obligations. The terms "assume" and "presuppose," when used by him in speaking of loving, may refer less to logical precursors, the groundwork of our conceptual grasp of the present state of those who are loved, than to how we must comport ourselves in loving. We must comport ourselves as if towards loving persons. Such an interpretation may put some strain on what is meant by 'assume' and 'presuppose,' but it is the sort of strain on the ordinary sense of things to which Kierkegaard was inclined, and I think that the strain causes no more discomfort than does the interpretation in terms of a potential to be loving.

Another possibility, and I think it a better one, is to see the assumption about others being loving as not necessarily about individuals who are being loved. It could be someone else altogether who is loving, and who thereby supports, or even makes possible, my act of loving the unloving person. Kierkegaard supports this view when he says in the same passage simply that I cannot be loving if I assume that I am the only loving person. The quality of being loving is not exclusive but is possible only on the assumption that I am a member of a loving community which includes at least one other person. This interpretation does more than just allow for Christian community; it stipulates that this basic spiritual quality is possible only in case there is a community.

If, then, community is required, and if indirect communication is possible and could be formative of such a community, the basic requirements of Christian existence as Kierkegaard defines it seem to be within reach. Walker locates Christian communication beyond the Socratic maieutic in indirectness, and sees this as impeding the formation of community, but why such special features of the Christian way as awareness of sin and the necessity of suffering intrinsically entail greater distance between individuals is not clear to me. In fact, the shift from the dialectical to the existential would seem to imply greater immediacy and directness, albeit more conflict.

Finally, I appreciate Walker's reminder that dying to the world does not take the individual out of the world in Kierkegaard's view. But then I would expect the deepened self-awareness that <u>is</u> involved to breech the insularity of isolated individualism and, at the least, allow for a multi-faceted world of human relationships which centre on Christian austerity but are refined rather than rendered impossible by it.

There are many more elements in Professor Walker's paper that deserve comment, but I cannot address myself to them today.

7

THE ETERNAL AS A SYNTHESIZING THIRD TERM IN KIERKEGAARD'S WORK

Maurice Carignan

In 1852, at a time when Kierkegaard's work had taken on an increasingly polemical complexion in his bitter struggle with the Christian establishment in Denmark,[1] he wrote in his Journals: "Man is a synthesis, and naturally, therefore, if you please, a born hypocrite, or with the possibility of being a hypocrite. And now God's concern with each individual is: Will you be a hypocrite or will you stand in relationship to truth?"[2]

Because of the opposing elements which synthesize him, man is both spiritual and sensual. The spiritual self gives an infinitely lofty meaning to the joy of Christianity. But the sensual self, pulling in the opposite direction, interprets this joy differently and, to the extent that it triumphs, hypocrisy is supreme.[3]

In another entry in his Journals, written two years later, he returned to the same idea: Man is a synthesis, a composite of the lower and the higher, and from birth on he is almost completely in the power of the lower . . . . Christianity is designed for the higher part of human nature, but in such a way that the lower nature will experience unhappiness because of it."[4]

These passages, along with others in the Journals touching on the subject of the human synthesis,[5] naturally recall The Concept of Dread from 1844. Vigilius Haufniensis, the pseudonymous author of that work, affirms there that man is "a synthesis of soul and body; but he is at the same time a synthesis of the temporal and the eternal."[6] The same passages reflect The Sickness Unto Death (1849) where Anti-Climacus goes still further: "Man is a synthesis of the infinite and the finite, of the temporal and the eternal, of freedom and necessity . . . ."[7]

When Kierkegaard and his pseudonymous authors describe man's nature in dialectic terms, it is in reaction to that substantialist thinking which had bogged down contemporary philosophical thought, and which in fact minimized the essential originality of the authentic self in its perpetual process of self-fulfilment.[8] Since man is indissolubly body and soul, finite and infinite, freedom and necessity, temporal and eternal, he harbours in his inmost being the ferment of his potential self, to be realized when his ideal self is related to his real self. Or, to put it more clearly, the self consists essentially of this very tension between the ideal and the real.

In the view of both Kierkegaard and his pseudonym Anti-Climacus, the self is identical with the path by which one becomes a Christian.[9] The embodiment of Christianity demonstrates the same attributes as the self and the soul: it is a process of becoming, an impetus, a ceaseless motion, running the perpetual risk of being false, illusory, hypocritical.

The exegeses of those passages in which Vigilius Haufniensis, Johannes Climacus, and Anti-Climacus define man is not easy, and those authors who have attempted it deserve much credit for their efforts.[10] Here, however, it is relevant to examine a difficulty of interpretation which one such author, Mark C. Taylor, has courageously brought out in his interesting book entitled Kierkegaard's Pseudonymous Authorship.[11]

1

Having defined man in terms of the polarities body-soul and temporal-eternal, Vigilius Haufniensis goes on to state: "The synthesis of the eternal and the temporal is not a second synthesis but is the expression for the first synthesis in consequence of which man is a synthesis of soul and body sustained by spirit. No sooner is the spirit posited than the instant is there."[12]

At first reading, this passage appears to affirm that there is a close parallel between the two syntheses, and even that they share the same real identity: the first, composed of body and soul, takes place in the spirit which is the third synthesizing force; the other effects in the instant the existential joining between temporal and eternal. The word Udtrykket (expression) used by Vigilius to define the relation between the two syntheses seems to suggest an equivalence between the body and the temporal, between the soul and the eternal, between the spirit and the instant. The same parallel could apply to the other two dialectical couplings enunciated later by Anti-Climacus: finite-infinite, necessity-possibility, where the synthesizing elements are, respectively, the self and freedom.[13]

The Concept of Dread also contains this further baffling statement: "The synthesis of the soulish and the bodily is to be posited by spirit, but the spirit is the eternal, and therefore this is accomplished only when the spirit posits at the same time along with this the second synthesis of the eternal and the temporal."[14]

Taylor effectively points out the difficulty of such a passage. The spirit, the synthesizing third term acting on the body-soul polarities, is identified with the eternal which in itself is a polarizing element of the temporal-eternal pair. It is not the soul that Vigilius identifies with the eternal, but the force which carries out the body-soul synthesis, that is, the spirit. Thus the parallelism which Vigilius' earlier statement seemed to claim no longer holds: the synthesis of the temporal and the eternal is not a simple literal translation of the body-soul synthesis. In fact, the same pseudonymous author earlier tacitly warned his readers against such a facile parallel when he said:

> As for the latter synthesis [i.e. of the temporal and the eternal], it evidently is not fashioned in the same way as the former. In the former case the two factors were soul and body and the spirit was a third term . . . . The other synthesis has only two factors: the temporal and the eternal. Where is the third term? And if there be no third term, there is really no synthesis; for a synthesis of that which is a contradiction cannot be completed as a synthesis without a third term. . . .[15]

Taylor attempts to solve the difficulty by saying that Vigilius Haufniensis' three statements must be taken literally.

This would allow a certain parallelism between the first and the second syntheses. But the equivalent of the temporal would be the pair of body and soul polarities in dialectic tension, which would at the same time be identical in reality to the two other pairs added by Anti-Climacus, finite and infinite, necessity and possibility. The synthesizing third term of these equivalent polarities would be identical to the eternal in the analogical sense of immobility, immutability, constancy. This would be freedom, a synthesizing force equivalent to the self and to the spirit. Thus, through the dialectic tension ruling his component parts, man would be settled in his temporality—equivalent to movement and to ontological anxiety. His freedom (his self, his spirit) would constitute the unchanging or eternal third force achieving the synthesis. The eternal, identical with freedom and with the spirit or the self, would constitute man in his essential temporality. And the instant would be permeated with eternity and eternity permeated with temporality.

If the self and the spirit can be identified with the eternal, it is through the instrument of freedom. Judge William, in Either/Or II, had earlier maintained the identity of the self and freedom: "But what, then, is this self of mine? If at the first instant I were to give the first expression for this, my answer is: It is the most abstract of all things, and at the same time it is the most concrete—it is freedom."[16]

And Anti-Climacus, the Christian extraordinarius of The Sickness Unto Death, echoes the words of the ethicist: "The self is composed of infinity and finiteness. But the synthesis is a relationship which, though it is derived, relates itself to itself, which means freedom. The self is freedom."[17] It would seem that this enlightening solution must be understood in the light of a clearly enunciated definition of freedom. It is useful here to examine the meaning with which Kierkegaard and his pseudonymous authors invested this word.

2

Holding forth on "the balance between esthetics and ethics" for the benefit of his friend Estheticist A (author of Either/Or I), Judge William points out that in philosophy, "There is an absolute of mediation," which is essential because "if we give up mediation, we give up speculation."

Yet, he wonders, is such a concession not dangerous? Would it not lead logically to the denial of an absolute choice, of an absolute dilemma? No, he replies, if one takes care not to confuse the domain of reason with the domain of freedom. In the first domain, opposition has no durability: it is mediated and passes over into a higher unity. But in the domain of freedom opposition can exist, being the alternative where one element excludes the other. The Judge continues: "I am by no means confounding liberum arbitrium with the genuine positive freedom, for this, too, has to all eternity evil outside itself, even if the evil be only an impotent possibility, and it does not become more perfect by more and more absorbing the evil but by more and more excluding it. But exclusion is precisely the opposition of mediation."[18]

This passage communicates the ethicist's conception of free will: contrary to genuine freedom, which affirms its positive character by excluding evil, free will—or the freedom to be indifferent—is negative in its nature, because its choice may settle alternatively on either good or evil. In his first draft of Philosophical Fragments in 1844, Kierkegaard followed the same train of thought: "Liberum arbitrium, which can equally well choose the good or the evil, is basically an abrogation of the concept of freedom and a despair of any explanation of it. Freedom means to be capable. Good and evil exist nowhere outside freedom, since this very distinction comes into existence through freedom."[19]

When compared and read together, the two texts maintain that true freedom, insofar as it exists at all, exists prior to free will, and means a capacity to tend toward perfection and therefore to exclude evil. He who would reduce freedom to free will, conceived as a balance between good and evil, would be committing an act of denial and debasing the concept.

Vigilius Haufniensis recalls the psychological origin of freedom. Speaking of "the religious genius . . . . who is not willing to stop with his immediateness," he says that "by the fact that he turns toward himself, he turns eo ipso toward God" and avows himself guilty. With penetrating clarity, he discovers sin in himself. But, by the same token, he also discovers freedom: "Freedom is his bliss, not freedom to do this or that in the world . . . . but freedom to know of himself that he is freedom."[20]

And yet, this religious genius, delighted to know that he himself is freedom, feels at the same moment the dread of sin, the dread of the potential sin which would rob him of freedom. And Vigilius goes on: "It is easily seen that freedom is not defiance by any means, or the selfish liberty understood in a finite sense. By such an assumption the effort has often been made to explain the origin of sin . . . . When freedom is so interpreted, its opposite is necessity . . . . No, the opposite of freedom is guilt."[21]

In other words, original sin has frequently been explained by the emergence of freedom, meaning by that the conscious possibility of disobedience or of a choice irremediably lodged in the finite. It was with great finesse and psychological perspicuity that Vigilius demonstrated the link between innocence, ignorance, and dread, and how the latter, in the bewilderment of freedom, was the psychological condition for the breach which was the first sin. "Dread," he said, "is freedom's reality as possibility for possibility."[22] In reality, it is impossible to explain the transition from innocence to sin: on the one hand, sin cannot have come into the world by necessity; on the other hand, neither can it stem from an abstract free will.[23] Before the breach occurs, freedom is only a possibility evoked by dread. Then: "To want to explain logically the entrance of sin into the world is a stupidity which could only occur to people who are comically anxious to get an explanation."[24] Vigilius is trying to stress the idea that true freedom is not by its very essence the opposite of the necessary. That would be what is commonly called free will, which thus conceived simply does not exist.[25] True freedom knows only one opposite: sin. It is essentially independence, freedom from bondage and from any link with sin. In this sense, a free man is not one who invariably and for an indefinite time possesses the power to choose between such and such courses of action, but rather the man who has acquired a second nature to guard him against sin. The prototype of the free man, the "religious genius," to revert to an expression of the ethicist William, is to break the circle of masked choices to enter into the realm of "eternal validity" where one learns to choose, with an ever-growing necessity, that which is contrary to sin.

Kierkegaard himself confirms this interpretation in several passages of his Journals. An entry dated 1850 demonstrates that Christianity imposes on man a primordial choice, that of the Kingdom of God, obliging him to shun the state of complete indifference which is free will. He continues: "Can there be a more accurate expression for the fact that freedom of choice is only a formal condition of freedom and that emphasizing freedom of choice as such means the sure loss of freedom? The content of freedom is decisive for freedom to such an extent that the very truth of freedom of choice is: there must be no choice, even though there is a choice."[26] The Christian, on pain of denying his own self must choose the one and only necessity, the Kingdom of God. "This," says the Christian, "is spirit."[27] It is true that this obligation would be unintelligible in itself if it did not presuppose the physical possibility of a contrary determination. It is physically possible for man to choose sin, that is, the finite, which contradicts the choice of the Kingdom of God. But, on the other hand, this choice must be eliminated to cede its place to the primordial option which is true freedom. This is unfortunately not often understood. "Precisely because men are a long way from being spirit, precisely therefore does freedom make so much trouble for them, since they continually remain suspended in freedom of choice. The reflection . . . . stares fixedly at freedom of choice instead of remembering that there must be no choice——and then choose."[28]

If true freedom tends to abolish choice, it is because the concrete self, the spirit, is capable of historicity. In 1851, Kierkegaard wrote: "That abstract freedom of choice is a phantasy, as if a human being at every moment of his life stood continually in this abstract possibility, so that consequently he never moves from the spot, as if freedom were not also an historical condition."[29]

Freedom, as far as it is identical with the self, with the spirit, has a history, and moves in a continuous becoming without which it would cease to exist. Kierkegaard explains through a simple comparison what this means. Because of the deliberation or rational thought process implied in the act of choosing a course of action, free will can be compared to a scale. Take the finest of all, he says, the one used to weigh gold. Its continued use constitutes its "history", a constantly more visible tendency, for example, to dip to one side or the other. And Kierkegaard continues: "So it is with the will. It has a history, a continually progressive history. A person can go so far that he finally loses even the capacity of being able to choose."[30] In the non-historic case of a person who had never made the conscious choice of himself and had always plunged deeper into sin by confining his "choices" to the finite sphere, such a state of slavery "is the punishment of sin . . . and is again sin."[31] This is the case with Don Juan, whose "freedom" is only indifference and vanity. In contrast, the person who freely shatters the sphere of estheticism, like Judge William, plunges thereby into a history, into the gradual formation of his self. There grows within him the necessity to choose the general. Having chosen himself in his eternal validity by eschewing the vain and the ephemeral, the ethicist is free. However, his freedom will not truly be on the road to perfection until his choices are made before God. Then will emerge the necessity to choose himself as an individual in conformity with his personal vocation, properly removed from esthetic seduction and the ethical general. Freedom, Kierkegaard says elsewhere, "goes through several stages before fully realizing itself."[32] That is its history, a gradual affirmation of necessity vis-à-vis the fundamental choice of the self as individual (Enkelte). Another passage of the Journals is even more explicit as to the affirmation of the bond between freedom and necessity: "What Augustine says of true freedom (distinguished from freedom of choice) is very true and very much a part of experience—namely, that a person has the most lively sense of freedom when with completely decisive determination he impresses upon his action the inner necessity which excludes the thought of another possibility. Then freedom of choice or the 'agony' of choice comes to an end."[33]

To summarize the position of Kierkegaard and his pseudonymous authors on the subject of freedom, we have the following:

1. True freedom excludes the moral possibility to choose evil, and can be found only at a positive level of man's progress toward perfection.
2. At this level, true freedom tends to blend with a certain necessity to affect the historicized will.
3. At that point free will no longer exists in the sense of a balancing factor, of indifference or of complete indetermination.
4. On the other hand, free will, understood as a physical capacity to choose, exists, at its best, as a great gift, but it threatens true freedom.

Given the fact that Kierkegaard[34] and his pseudonym

Vigilius Haufniensis[35] appeal to the authority of Leibniz to reject free will,[36] it could be deduced that their implicit stand is one of a closed psychological determinism.[37] This, however, seems not to be so. How can one understand the analyses of Judge William and of Vigilius Haufniensis without taking for granted that they believe in man's freedom to choose? Moreover, the Journals entry just cited explicitly admits that such freedom exists and is a great gift bestowed on man: "Usually the freedom of being able to choose is represented as an extraordinary good. This it is, but it nevertheless depends also upon how long it is going to last. Usually one makes the mistake of thinking that this itself is the good and that this freedom of choice lasts one's entire life."[38]

3

At this point, we know that for the pseudonyms Vigilius Haufniensis and Anti-Climacus—and most probably for Kierkegaard himself—the synthesizing thirds, self, spirit and freedom, are one single reality identical to the eternal, an element of a supreme synthesis realized in the instant. We also know that, in their view, freedom implies degrees of autonomy or independence, of which the lowest—and the one most likely to disappear in favour of the highest level—is free will or free choice.

This is the time to examine the meaning which Taylor attributes to the word freedom when, in his exegesis, he identifies it with the self, with the spirit, with the eternal.

Taking up the difficult statement of Anti-Climacus to the effect that "the self is a relation which relates itself to its own self,"[39] he interprets it, and rightly in our opinion, as meaning: the self is a relation which relates its ideal, potential, infinite self to its real, actual, finite self.[40] This interpretation has great merit in that it stresses the tension, the dynamism, and the becoming which in Kierkegaard's eyes and in the view of his pseudonyms constitute the very essence of the self. To relate the ideal self to the real self is to enter fully into the painful process of giving to the self the perfection due its very nature as a human.

It is true that this activity, the self building itself, cannot be carried out without the exercise of free will, without freedom of choice. In truth, it is inconceivable that the self could transmute ideality into reality without having to make the essential choice of its self, without choosing choice instead of tending, like estheticist A, toward an impossible and total abstention.[41] But to define the precise meaning of this freedom which is identified with the eternal, we must first, with Taylor, refer to the meaning taken on by this latter term, "eternal."

It cannot be claimed that the eternity of the self or of the spirit is the same as the eternity of God. Kierkegaard and his pseudonyms have too much of a belief in divine transcendence to hold such a view. The term has to be understood as an analogy. Immutability, immobility may be used analogically in referring to God or to man. Man lives in the temporal because his possibilities and his reality are in perpetual movement. But his eternity, that which in him remains constant and unchangeable, is his freedom. Taylor defines this freedom as "the capacity to take some course of action."[42] The determination itself or the course of action can vary, of course, but the capacity which underlies it is invariable, unchangeable, eternal.

It would seem that it is a question of a pure and simple capacity for choice. It is unfortunate that our commentator has not demonstrated how this conception of the eternal in man meshes with the Kierkegaard imperative so often proclaimed: to become the spirit, to become the eternal. In other words, how can it be our duty to become freedom in the sense of the capacity to take a course of action?

The answer, according to the exceptionally Christian Anti-Climacus, is that it is definitely a question of duty. Further, it is an agonizing duty, as Kierkegaard claims in his Journals in 1851: "If we, in our present way of life, are to be truthful before God, we would have to talk like this: I understand very well that to become spirit is really the requirement, but could you not grant me a little indulgence . . . . I would so much like to enjoy the things of this earth and, Lord God, I do not pretend to be stronger than I am——I am only a child."[43] Further, and especially in the last years of his life, the Danish thinker expressed forcefully and almost pitilessly the requirements of Christianity, of which the most basic was to become spirit. The Journals from 1854 contain resounding statements like the following: "Spirit is restlessness; Christianity is the most profound restlessness of existence——so it is in New Testament. In Christendom Christianity is tranquilization 'so that we can really enjoy life.'"[44] "God (according to Christianity) does not want men to have tranquillity——spirit is restlessness."[45] "To become a Christian, according to the New Testament, is to become 'spirit.' To become spirit, according to the New Testament, is to die, to die to the world."[46] As he clearly says in On My Work as an Author, Kierkegaard's mission was precisely to denounce the illusion of a facile, convenient, static Christianity.[47]

As for Anti-Climacus, he is fierce in his judgement of any false Christian: "The soulish-bodily synthesis in every man is planned with a view to being spirit, such is the building; but the man prefers to dwell in the cellar, that is, in the determinants of sensuousness . . . ."[48] Given the equivalence of the realities of the spirit, the self, freedom and eternity, one must conclude that freedom is for man an ideal to be realized, a duty to be accomplished. But what does this mean concretely?

One possible interpretation[49] would be that man has the duty and the responsibility to acquire the capacity to choose his own course of action despite the false imperatives of a world living in illusion. But is this capacity not already there, at the moment of the spirit's first palpitations at the approach of dread? Is it not at least potentially the attribute of each human synthesis of body and soul? How can we be obliged to acquire what we already have? Also, Judge William's contention that man is obliged to "choose himself" or to choose choice means something quite different . . . . Such statements, like those of Vigilius Haufniensis and Anti-Climacus, are difficult to understand without the presupposition of such a capacity in every man, even in the most sensual of estheticists. Where the capacity does not exist, one cannot see the possibility of its arising, except through creative action. As the Judge says: "For in case what I chose did not exist but absolutely came into existence with the choice, I would not be choosing, I would be creating; but I do not create my self, I choose my self."[50]

Another interpretation could be that man, being the very immediate synthesis of body and soul, has within himself a capacity for choice which it is his duty to exercise instead of leaving it indefinitely in a state of dream or of pure potentiality. At first glance, this solution has a certain attraction: Estheticist A, who is being attacked by the Judge, is after all the prototype of the person who tends to abstain from choice, even while he masks his very abstention. When the twelve strokes of midnight sound and the hour comes to remove the masks—— to use the Judge's metaphor—— then his characteristic non-engagement will be revealed. But at the same time we also see that he could never succeed in avoiding choice completely: to abstain from choice is still a choice. Only the repetition of choice will have been avoided: unlike the ethicist who chooses choice, the estheticist chooses not to choose. To choose pleasure, no matter how it is refined or how it is masked, is not to choose, except in the figurative sense as the Judge says,[51] because: "But he who says that he wants to enjoy life always posits a condition which either lies outside the individual or is in the individual in such a way that it is not posited by the individual himself."[52] There is no doubt that for Judge William the estheticist in general and by his very nature cannot be involved in the constituent becoming of the self or of the spirit because of his very incapacity to choose choice or to intensify his choice. This is the same conclusion expressed by Anti-Climacus and Kierkegaard himself, as has been seen. The inauthentic Christians whom they unmask have not chosen themselves as spirit, but live in the sphere of esthetic illusion and its masked choices.

Now if the duty to become freedom were nothing more than the obligation to actualize the capacity for choice, the estheticist in general who chooses pleasure—— even the pleasure provided by illusion——would invariably respond to this requirement.

Thus it behooves us to point out that the freedom to choose can never touch the eternal element in man except insofar as it orients his actions toward ethical and religious perfection.

It has just been shown, however, that for Kierkegaard this capacity to choose is destined to become blurred as man reaches his own realization as spirit——or as freedom. In other words, the more real freedom grows within man, the more rapidly will his capacity to choose dwindle to give way to an internal necessity which puts an end to the agony of decision.[53] Freedom of choice, therefore, is not identical with the immobile, unchangeable quality which is the eternal in man. It is rather a necessary but temporary measure used to reach the eternal. The interior necessity which eventually replaces it——like the furrow of a concrete course of action, dug by choice——will be the manifestation of a freedom finally made reality.

To reach a conclusion: instead of being the simple possibility of choice or the very actualization of such a possibility, freedom, as a third synthesizing term identical to the eternal, is rather a call to existence. "What is existence?" wonders Johannes Climacus in The Postscript. And he replies: "Existence is the child that is born of the infinite and the finite, the eternal and the temporal, and is therefore a constant striving."[54] It is through effort, through lack of tranquillity, through the pain of birth, that man must grow as a temporal being, that is, as a synthesis in the process of actualizing the equivalent pairs of infinite and finite, of possibility and necessity, of soul and body. To achieve this synthesis is to pass over from the immediate into the eternal; it is to become one's own self; it is to exist.

The dynamic presence of the eternal in man cannot be expressed in a univocal manner but allows of every possible degree of analogy. The task of achieving self-realization is never finished.

At the bottom of the ladder, on various rungs, one finds the estheticist for whom eternity remains an unanswered appeal, a vain quest for liberation. Judge William gives a masterful description of Nero's masked torment when faced with the entreaties of the eternal: "The spirit constantly desires to break through, but it cannot attain the metamorphosis, it is constantly disappointed, and he would offer it the satiety of pleasure. Then the spirit within him gathers like a dark cloud, its wrath broods over his soul, and it becomes an anguishing dread which erases not even in the moment of pleasure."[55] The eyes are the mirrors of the soul. But when we consider Nero, "behind the eye lies the soul as a gross darkness."[56] The basically childish caprices of this man are extravagant, cruel, and monstrous because the spirit, continually denied, ceaselessly haunts him. The eternal within him, the source of his confusion, remains in the state of pure potentiality. Nero refuses to embark on the painful odyssey which would affirm his freedom, where his ideal self would relate to his real self. He refuses to accept the joint penetration of the temporal and the eternal into the instant. Or, to repeat the Judge's felicitous phrase, he refuses to give birth to himself through the creative effort of his will.[57]

The bursting of the sphere where the spirit is enchained can be achieved only through a redoubled choice, the choice of choice, or the absolute choice of the self. Man himself chooses himself when, unlike Don Juan or Nero, he chooses the painful becoming which makes him spirit, as he becomes one with the general.

But ethical liberation would also be an illusion if it blocked the constituent movement of the spirit or of the eternal in search of itself. The sphere of the general must also burst to allow the self to climb a rung higher, the rung of the religious person. Freedom will have reached its highest point when man has chosen himself as a Christian. But at that point he will have reached the point of profoundest anxiety, the fear and trembling which no Christian can ever escape without becoming a hypocrite.

Comment on Carignan

Peter Carpenter

There are two main themes in this paper: man as synthesis, and man as free. In dealing with them, the paper makes use of the theories developed by Mark Taylor, in his book Kierkegaard's Pseudonymous Authorship. I will briefly summarize the arguments and will attempt as far as I can to clarify the central issues. And in the course of this analysis I will raise one or two questions of my own.

I Man as Synthesis

Kierkegaard uses various expressions to describe this synthesis: body/soul, temporal/eternal, finite/infinite, necessity/possibility. In all of these cases there is of course a third synthesizing factor: body/soul (spirit), temporal/eternal (instant), finite/infinite (self), necessity/possibility (freedom). At first glance these seem like parallel expressions, but Kierkegaard soon shatters this illusion when, in The Concept of Dread, he identifies "spirit" and "the eternal". "Spirit" was said to be the third factor synthesizing body and soul, while "the instant" was seen as the third factor uniting "the temporal" and "the eternal". Why then does Kierkegaard equate spirit and eternal? If C synthesizes A and B, and if Z synthesizes X and Y, one would expect C to be equated with Z. Kierkegaard, however, equates C and Y.

Taylor's solution is to take the "temporal" from the temporal/eternal synthesis and to equate this with the polarities, body and soul, and also with the other two polarities—finite and infinite, necessity and possibility. Thus the eternal, which unites with the temporal in the instant, becomes equivalent to the other three synthesizing factors; in other words, the eternal is identified with spirit, self, and freedom. The temporal and the eternal were seen as forming a synthesis in the instant; so now these other syntheses are likewise seen as occurring in the instant.

What we have then is an equation of eternal, spirit, self, and freedom. But in what sense is man (as spirit or self or freedom) eternal? Carignan points out that a distinction must be made between the self as eternal and God as eternal.[58] Eternity, when predicated by man, he says, must be understood "analogically." One could put this another way, perhaps, by distinguishing between the eternal as immanent and the eternal as transcendent. Kierkegaard, for example, talks about the transcendent eternal in a comment on reduplication. "Real self-reduplication without a third factor, which is eternal and compels one, is an impossibility . . . . The transformation which really lies in changing from immediacy to spirituality, . . . becomes in fact an illusion, . . . if there is not some third and compelling factor, which is not the individual himself."[59]

II Man as Free

The paper now focuses on the question of freedom. Using Taylor as a point of departure, Carignan shows how Kierkegaard distinguishes between free will or freedom of choice, and "true freedom."

1. Freedom of choice

Taylor makes two points: first, that freedom is eternal. (This is based on the interpretation of the Kierkegaardian synthesis according to which, as we saw, the eternal was identified with spirit, self, and freedom.) Freedom is eternal, Taylor explains, in the sense that it is unchanging and constant.[60] Carignan's criticism here is that Taylor does not relate the conception of this unchanging, constant, eternal freedom to the view of Kierkegaard that one has to become spirit, to become eternal.[61] Taylor simply talks as if man were eternal, whereas Kierkegaard sees this rather as a task, not as a fait accompli.

Taylor's second point is that freedom is the capacity to take some course of action. In other words, freedom is the freedom to choose. What does this mean? Carignan asks:

-that one should acquire the capacity to choose? No, because when Judge William in Either/Or talks of "choosing oneself" or "choosing to choose," he presupposes the freedom to determine one's own course of action.

-does it then mean that one should develop one's innate capacity to choose? Again, no. To understand it this way is to concede too much to the aesthete whose refusal to choose is really a choice. (He chooses not to choose.) According to Judge William this doesn't constitute a real becoming. Merely possessing or developing the capacity to choose is not a true exercise of freedom.

Carignan's conclusion is that the freedom to choose is only eternal to the degree that it is oriented towards ethical and religious perfection.[62]

Freedom to choose, however, is seen only as preliminary or provisional. One must advance beyond this to "true freedom." But before discussing this let us first consider the four-fold distinction in the meaning of freedom as outlined in the Westminster Confession of Faith (1647). (Not only is this a most helpful analysis, it also expresses the kind of outlook that moulded Kierkegaard's own thinking on this question.)

-the state of innocence (original righteousness): man "had freedom and power to will and to do that which is good." This is the freedom of posse non peccare.

-the state of sin (state of nature): man, now a fallen creature, is utterly unable to will what is good. He is free only in the minimal sense of having a will.

-the state of grace: with God's help man can freely choose and will what is good.

-the state of glory: the "will of man is made perfectly and immutably free to do good." This is the greater freedom of non posse peccare.

In the light of these distinctions, let us see how Carignan elaborates Kierkegaard's conception of "true freedom."

2. True Freedom

a. True freedom is the contrary of sin. This of course

echoes Romans 14:23 " . . . whatever does not proceed from faith is sin."

b. True freedom is characterized by necessity. An "inner necessity" impels the individual into a certain course of action and in so doing excludes all other possibilities. This, as Kierkegaard says, is "the most lively sense of freedom" a man can have.[63] The "state of glory" will bring such freedom to perfection, but until that day other possibilities do in fact remain, possibilities of evil. This is why, as Carignan puts it: the religious genius, who delights in his freedom, "feels at the same moment the dread of sin, the dread of the potential sin which would rob him of his freedom".[64] Carignan does draw attention to this element of anxiety in freedom, but he does not emphasize it sufficiently. This is evident particularly in his summary of Kierkegaard's understanding of freedom. No mention is made of guilt and sin!

c. True freedom means advancing beyond the ethical to the religious.[65] Freedom must attain this highest stage, and yet even here one cannot escape "fear and trembling." This is another reminder of the fact that, as Luther says, man is _simul peccator et justus_. Kierkegaard's theology of freedom is therefore not a theology of glory (in spite of his talk of the "necessity" of freedom) but a theology of man _en route_ to glory.[66]

8

TWO LEVELS OF INDIRECT COMMUNICATION: LANGUAGE AND 'LEGEND' IN MARK 6

H. A. Nielsen

Mark 6:45-52 is, on the face of it, a turbulence-anecdote like most, though not quite all, of the narratives in the gospels which speak of turbulence in private lives, in official circles Jewish and Roman, in urban and rural settings, in sea and sky, occasionally even in sealed tombs. For the most part the evangelists let the moments of turbulence speak for themselves. How then does this moment of turbulence, a man walking on water, speak?

Start with the most elementary aspect of the text, its immediate content. While the spectacle might not disturb the rhythm of a cow's mandible, a man walking on water is doing something men can't do, and the disciples in the boat, Mark tells us, are buffaloed, terrified. No one needs faith to grasp that a walker on the waves, no matter how like us he might be, is in that respect as unlike us as a long-legged bug scooting on the surface of a pond. An enormous difference strikes the naked eye, though not perhaps a cow's eye, when we confront the immediate content of Mark 6. Of course it is possible to call the narrative 'legend' and thus place ourselves in the company of some well-known scripture scholars, Protestant, Anglican, and Catholic,[1] but we have not yet finished letting it speak to us. Prior to any such judgment I can feel primitively puzzled by the fact that I don't even have a name for the difference between me and a man who can do what humans can't do. If a name for that difference is not too much to ask, where would I look for it except in the same source where the narrative occurs? As it happens, if we look further we do in fact find a name for the difference in quite a few places: sin. Not the most fathomable word in the world or the most fashionable, but it keeps turning up.

Now a curious twist begins to appear. The difference, the sole difference between the walker on the waves and me, is called sin. But then am I being told that except for sin I, too, could walk on water and do the other things in Mark 6 that humans can't do, multiply loaves of bread and kill whole armies of germs with my bare hands? The fact of the matter is, I have no well-formed idea of what I could do if it were not for sin, no clear idea of what power sources if any I could tap into at will except for sin. And while we are on the subject, what is sin? By putting our earlier question to Mark 6, we seem to be led to a sense of the term 'sin' that points beyond what people the world over call sins or evildoings. Kierkegaard, not independently of the New Testament and the Christian tradition, calls sin "an existence-determinant, and precisely one which cannot be thought."[2] Particular sins are something a human being can think, i.e., plan, consciously commit, later recall, and so forth. However, a determinant of the whole of my existence could not be thought, could not for example be discovered by cogitation, since my thinking capacity along with the rest of me would be dyed with the same dye.[3]

If every human were in fact in such an unthinkable, all-enveloping state, how would anyone ever become aware of it? As we keep that question in mind, the curious twist I spoke of appears in this way: underneath the immediate content of Mark 6 lies a further content that comes to light as I let the immediate lead me into conversation with other parts of the book. A mediate content comes into view: a sin-message, the intimation of an unperceivable state that holds me fast. In Mark 6 this mediate content reveals my state by means of a contrast with someone who is not in that state, a sinless one, as other texts in the New Testament assert directly. Who would have imagined that a man walking on water would call to mind an unthinkable condition in the rest of us instead of just in himself? Who would have surmised that such a condition is what makes water-wings a must for children at the beach? We have no secular basis for connecting the fact that we can drown with anything beyond the reach of thought.

Mark 6 makes no mention of sin. This suggests that one function of the language of Mark 6 is to uncover and impart an indirect message by drawing the reader into a colloquy touched off by the direct content. And drawing him gently——for if I am in a state repellent to whatever powers made me, no doubt they could really rub my nose in it, for example by making me hideous to myself. But instead a man walks on the waves——and sin is not mentioned. The presence of an indirect content helps explain why so many searching minds over the centuries have experienced no difficulty ingesting a text such as Mark 6, despite its stubbornly opaque element. Normally, that is, people are positioned to receive indirect material along with the direct. I am not suggesting, of course, that the mind of the typical reader operates in precisely the sequence I have described. My point is that the average reader does not start from the hard-line premise that the gospels communicate directly and in no other way; consequently a number of difficulties which critical scholarship finds in the surface layer of a text such as Mark 6 strike the ordinary reader as simply unreal.

So far, I take it, nothing like faith is involved in these remarks, but only (a) reading an anecdote of turbulence, (b) noticing the immediate content, (c) observing that it alludes to a sharp difference between me and the walker on the waves, (d) tracking down a name for the difference, and (e) allowing a mediate or indirect content to unfold. Merely being made somewhat aware of an unthinkable state is a long way from putting it behind me, repenting, receiving faith, or however we please to express it. "But you couldn't get this far in your colloquy with the gospel," someone objects, "unless you did more than read that he walked on the water. You also have to believe that he did so, and despite your disclaimer this means you bring faith into your reading." ——It is worth a pause to examine the misunderstanding here. What does the objector mean by believing the anecdote? Actually I can do very little with an account of a hopelessly baffling performance other than put baffled questions to it such as, "How come he can but I can't?" I cannot prove or disprove that the event happened; I can't assimilate it into a clear skein of historical prose, since it throws a block to the understanding; nor can I repeat the performance. The most I can do is let the text take me by the dialectical hand and lead me, via my own queries, to other texts which happen to be present in the same source and happen to say something unexpected about my state. The objector has confused believing the text with giving it a hearing. Giving it a hearing means letting it unfold its indirect content (if any) in response to my questions, since its direct content is as much of a nonplus to me as Mark says it was to the men in the boat.

From what we have noted it would appear that reading the text, as opposed to scanning it, inspecting it, and the like, requires of me that I do not choke off the flow of indirect content. I dare not assume that the immediate content conveys all that the text has to say. Where that assumption prevails in scripture scholarship, a staid intelligence will see the walking on water account as religious foolishness or myth in a damaging sense, while a more pliant intelligence sees it as ecstatic overstatement, poetry, metaphor, or myth in a softer sense. Inevitably the text will withhold its indirect payload from any reader who works under that assumption.

To summarize, the language of Mark 6 works by first presenting a turbulence-anecdote containing a baffling element, which in turn has a function: it apprises the reader of a so far nameless difference between himself and the walker on the waves. By allowing this to lead or draw him into other corners of the source, he becomes aware of an indirect disclosure of his own condition back in Mark 6. This disclosure takes place not in the only possible way, but by a contrast in which sin and sinlessness are alike presented in shielded light. Further natural questions such as, 'How serious is this condition?' lead by zigs and zags to the narrative of the Passion, among others. All of this adds up, it seems to me, to a supple and powerful mode of communication, a mixture of direct and indirect, of veiling and disclosure, offering guidance to a reader who allows the text to speak its baffling piece, yet at the same time stretching a trip-wire across the path of anyone who assumes that the direct content is all that it has to offer. Whether one is inclined to call it a singular mode of communication or not, the like of it is not easy to find.

Prepared to call a halt at this point, I kept hearing

the voices of three scripture scholars, one German, one British, one American, all saying of Mark 6, "Legend, legend, legend." Consider the following remarks, versions of which may be found in dozens of contemporary works of scholarship: "Legends such as the story about walking on water attached themselves to historical material as the early church sought to express its post-Easter faith in the commanding personality that proclaimed the Kingdom. Today we can discern the same proclamation even as we discount the face-value of that mythical overlay." Whatever else may be said of the message received by people who talk this way, it certainly does not include the disclosure of an unthinkable contrast between Jesus and themselves. To stand pat with 'personality' difference such as a self-assured or authoritative manner of speaking relativizes sin into an eminently thinkable condition. At any rate this bit of scholarly convergence on the lengendary nature of Mark 6 led me to look again at that complex, layered communication.

Something I had missed began now to stand out. If there was a condition that colored the mental as well as other dimensions of human life, what sort of contrast would offer us at least a glimpse, the beginning of an awareness, of its hold on us? Only an unthinkable contrast, it would seem, one which would arrest thought like a shot of novocain in the frontal lobe. Without pretending to guess the various forms this might take, though it is easy to imagine one or two that would more than unnerve the beholder, we can say that one such contrast is given in the immediate content of Mark 6 and a number of other texts which represent a man doing the humanly unrepeatable. On the other hand, if the texts presented no content that was (a) bound up with life-or-death matters and (b) incogitable or mind-blocking, we would have no occasion or incentive to unpack a mediate content having to do with an unthinkable condition. The humanly unrepeatable element in texts such as Mark 6 is therefore an indispensable conduit for indirect content of that nature, which cannot be put across as information on a flat trajectory, like a stock market report, but only by ricocheting off a contrast between ourselves and a sinless one. In this respect the direct and the indirect content of Mark 6 are strikingly adapted to each other.

It was evident, however, that none of this spoke decisively to the question of legend. Then in the space of two or three days something dawned which for me put the whole gospel mode of communication in a morning light. To begin with, the accessibility of an indirect content disclosing a state which men could not discover on their own is of more than passing significance for a reader. Next, as we have noted, the immediate and the indirect or mediate content of Mark 6 are mutually supportive. In other words, without some such immediate content (not necessarily walking on water but a contrast of that kind), an unthinkable condition could not be disclosed within the limitation discussed earlier, i.e., short of a full frontal assault on man's senses. Similarly, without a corresponding mediate content to illuminate and characterize that condition, the immediate account would stand mute. Together the direct and indirect form a whole articulation, and between them the light plays.

Now comes a further twist, more than merely curious. The fact that an indirect content, matching up with the direct content, is there to be found invalidates doubts of the direct content, and thus by a second movement of indirection certifies the historicity, not of walking on water specifically, but of some performance beyond the continuum of human striving, some performance that slides right off the graph-paper. The act of setting one's face against the historicity of Mark 6 for whatever reasons, instantly screens from sight the indirect content, which if allowed into daylight has a way of drawing attention to itself and away from the merely occasioning immediate content. The reasons offered for calling Mark 6 a legend add up to the claim that there is something offensive about it as it stands, that it can't be literally true, that it bears the stamp of a credulous age, that it echoes the Old Testament, and similar things. However, reading the direct content, unless it is done with openness to indirect material, amounts only to sweep-scanning the text, no matter how systematically or learnedly one scans. If I pronounce the direct material a legend, the accessibility of an indirect content, commensurate with the direct and summoned forth by it, indicts me for a balk, not a doubt, for I didn't finish reading Mark 6 before breaking off with it.

We are obliged, then, to add a further note to our earlier description of the way the language of Mark 6 functions: our access to a mediate content does not prove the historicity of the immediate content (which after all concerns earthly contingent matters such as human bodies, water, a boat), but invalidates any doubts of a sort that would choke off the indirect content; it does this by exposing them ironically as balks, as offense. Access to the mediate does prove, however, that the humanly unrepeatable happened in some form or other, since the humanly unrepeatable is an indispensable vehicle for communicating precisely that indirect material. If instead it took the form of, say, a man sleeping comfortably in a raging fire, would anything be gained by changing the story to one of walking on water? (Notice, though, that even if this account holds up under criticism, it would be absurd to conclude from it that the historicity of biblical narratives should never be questioned, contested, or doubted, or that all such doubts are balks. Certain texts, Mark 6 for one, may carry a hidden stinger against standing doubts or denials of their historicity, but a great many other texts do not.)

The direct, baffling, 'foolish' content leads to the indirect disclosure of an unthinkable condition, which in turn—incidentally—certifies in a general way the integrity of the original direct content! Have we any other book that puts the simplest kind of language through paces like these? The whole mode of communication, in its dynamism, seems to me to go well beyond our notions of mastery, virtuosity, and genius. The language breathes and pulses, yet can play dead when a shadow passes over it. Foolishness turns into something else before our eyes. Rudely simple prose opens like an oiled casement to one who puts natural questions to it, but sticks shut to one who merely examines it through strong lenses. Straightforward and simple in its composition, as communication it seems packed with measureless mentality, pains, and tension. A humanly unrepeatable deed becomes an avenue to instruction, and then the instruction casually visits its blessing on the unrepeatable performance! This confronts us, I believe, with something unparalleled in the sphere of linguistic expression: a less than elegant-looking edifice of words, marked by a variety of human smudges, yet capable of any flexure of a living intelligence——and then some. My first reaction to this, apart from amazement, was the strong feeling that the analysis had gone haywire somewhere. No one in his right mind would set out to prove that events analogous to walking on water happened, if only because there is no species of reasoning we could call into service for that purpose. Yet it seems to me now that something very like a silencer of doubts has emerged, wholly unexpectedly, in the form of quiet backlash against a certain way of reading Mark 6, namely by halves.

This brings us to a touchy subject: the mind behind the gospels. If in fact the accessibility of indirect material related to Mark 6 voids doubts as to the historicity of the direct content, then that narrative (within its New Testament setting, of course) has a surprising and remarkable feature. But whose linguistic achievement are we talking about? Whose mentality? If I say it is the mind of God, I go beyond describing how gospel language works and start explaining in a pother of speculation, helpless to back up my words. Language in the gospels is indeed so deployed as to permit those extraordinary flexures. However, to avoid falling into a mystification here, we should keep in mind that apart from its use the gospel language is just as inert as any other. It needs a reader for the divulgence of its indirect content, a reader who will hold up his end of a conversation with, not about, the New Testament. Yet if, despite its simplicity, the gospel language possesses those qualitatively distinct laminae, all adapted to an integral articulation, must we remain tongue-tied concerning the mind behind that language? Consider the task of composing a piece of writing which includes these features:

1. a brief narrative in a larger setting, told in language simple enough to be passed on orally from one unschooled generation to the next;
2. the narrative tells of a roughly dateable but scientifically incomprehensible event;
3. under questioning the narrative in its wider setting delivers an indirect personal message which meshes with the incomprehensible in 2;
4. the presence of the indirect message authenticates as historical the incomprehensible event or its like.

This is by no means a full description of how the language of Mark 6 works, but as a partial sketch it serves our limited purpose. The task of coming up with a piece of writing that meets those four specifications is so far beyond the resources of authors I am familiar with, including a few highly resourceful ones, that the ideas of someone consciously composing it strip the gears of imagination.

Perhaps, then, one could turn to hyperconscious or ecstatic authorship, but in the absence of an actual example that comes close to meeting those specifications, the suggestion lacks force. For these reasons the safest thing one can say about the mind behind the gospels is the confession: I for one cannot make words and sentences perform so athletically. To press further, it seems to me, would be to look for the mind behind the gospels in the sphere of speculation rather than in the gospels themselves. As we have been observing, the gospels, mainly in their indirect content, offer their own answers to questions about the mind behind them. What else are we glimpsing when, for example, and to begin with, we detect a concern to reveal an unthinkable condition, and to do it tenderly?

Again, to regard these observations as being in any sense an expression of Christian faith would wipe out the distinction between reading a text, or giving it, as we say, a decent hearing, and on the other hand responding by worshipping Christ as Lord. Today as in New Testament times the sin-message is essentially an overture, the mere hearing of which neither presupposes that the hearer is a disciple nor turns him into one. To read fully is an expression not of Christian faith but of good faith, and to identify Christian faith with good faith is, in my opinion, bad faith.

Comment on Nielsen

David Lochhead

Professor Nielsen has provided us with a philosophico-theological meditation on the story of Jesus walking on the water. As stimulating as I found the paper, I have major difficulties with at least three points. These are the exegesis of Mark 6, the nature of the historical-critical method, and the distinction between direct and indirect communication. In order to keep this response within reasonable bounds, I will concentrate on one point only: the distinction between direct and indirect communication.

Professor Nielsen claims that a reading of Mark 6 leads to a sense of amazement. Why amazement? Because I cannot walk on water. There must be some difference between me and Jesus. But how can I name that difference? The answer, Professor Nielsen claims, is "sin". Sin, of course, is not mentioned in the text. The conclusion, "I am a sinner," must have been communicated indirectly.

Then, according to Nielsen, there is a second level of indirection. Our awareness of sin has been awakened by one whom we find to be unique. Thus if Jesus did not walk on water, he must have done something like it.

The argument is, of course, more subtle than that. I hope that I have presented it fairly, if not completely. If this is Professor Nielsen's argument, I am inclined to agree with the remark of one of my more perceptive students who described this as an ontological argument for the historicity of miracle stories.

I suspect that Professor Nielsen and I have very

different understandings of what constitutes the difference between direct and indirect communication. In my understanding of Kierkegaard, which on this point derives primarily from Concluding Unscientific Postscript and Training in Christianity, a kind of analogy can be established: Objectivity is to Subjectivity as direct communication is to indirect communication. Direct communication is what pertains to objective facts. Indirect communication is what pertains to subjective or existential truth. Direct communication changes your mind. Indirect communication changes your life.

If that generalization of the distinction is sound, I fear that Professor Nielsen has confused the distinction between direct and indirect communication with another one. I would describe Professor Nielsen's argument as distinguishing explicit and implicit communication.

I was struck on first reading the paper how easily sin enters the picture. It is not mentioned in the text. Nielsen's argument depends on that. But as I read the text I am told that its meaning is bound up with the text which immediately precedes it: the miracle of the loaves and fishes. Mark 6:51b-52 reads, "The disciples were completely amazed, because they had not understood what the loaves of bread meant; their minds could not grasp it." Yet there is not a word about this in Nielsen's derivation of the concept of sin.

I wondered for a while why Professor Nielsen had dealt with Mark to the exclusion of the parallel passage in Matthew 14:22-33. Yet if we examine the text in Matthew, the answer seems clear. In Matthew Jesus was not alone in walking on the water. Peter joined him. The message there is insofar as you have faith, you can walk on water. The "difference" is faith. Peter's faith fails. The faith of Jesus did not fail. The conclusion, explicit in the passage, is that Jesus does not fail because he is the Son of God. The implicit communication here is not about sin but about the reality of the Incarnation.

The immediate context of the incident of Jesus walking on the water contains clues to its "meaning." Nielsen does not appeal to the immediate context. His conclusion that there is a difference between me and the one who walks on water is drawn from a wider context, namely the witness of the New Testament as a whole to the person of Jesus Christ. In that context there can be no argument. "Sin" is one of the terms used in the New Testament to describe the way in which Jesus is uniquely different from the rest of us. Surely looking at a text in context still involves one in the objective reading of a text. I fail to see that Nielsen's reader who gives a "decent reading" to the text differs significantly from Kierkegaard's ecclesiastic who proposes subjects for reflection at the foot of the cross. Both are bound to the truth objectively understood if implicitly communicated. The recognition that sin is implied by the text does not force us to a decision about repentance.

The discovery of sin is Nielsen's first level of indirection. His second level would lead us to an invalidation of doubts about the historicity of the text. He does not argue for the historicity of this particular incident. Rather he argues that a unique (i.e. sinless) individual must have performed unique acts like walking on the water. The uniqueness of the act cannot invalidate the account.

I find it somewhat remarkable that an argument like this should be put at a conference devoted to the work of Kierkegaard without an admission that something basic to Kierkegaard was being rejected. Proof, even the soft kind of proof which Nielsen advances, is consistently rejected by Kierkegaard. For Climacus/Kierkegaard, proving is an activity which belongs solely to direct communication. Indirect communication leads not to an invalidation of doubts but to the possibility of offense. The latter category is completely lacking in Nielsen's exposition. The historical-critical scholars whose judgment of "legend" Nielsen so adamantly rejects are not presented as taking offense at Christ. Rather, he suggests, they are allowing scientific prejudice to exclude a scientifically incomprehensible event.

My difficulty with Nielsen's second level of indirection is essentially the same as my objection to his first level. In both his discovery of sin and in his proof of the historicity of "something like" walking on water Nielsen never leaves the realm of objectivity and results. The text speaks only directly. Indirection never appears, let alone reaches two levels!

The reason that indirect communication does not appear is related to Nielsen's decision to bracket the question of faith. He is dealing with the problem of being open to the text rather than reading the text as an expression of Christian faith. That is a perfectly appropriate question to raise. Is it possible, for example, for me to be able to be open to a text of the Pali Canon without putting my Christian commitment on the line? This is an important question, but it is doubtful that Kierkegaard's category of indirect communication would be helpful in formulating a hermeneutical theory to deal with that type of openness. What I can infer from a text and how I am changed by it are distinguishable questions. It is the former question Nielsen deals with. It is the latter which involves indirect communication.

I think that it would be possible to speak of indirect communication in this text apart from faith. It would be indirect communication, for example, if, as a result of reading this text, the attempt to walk on water became the passion of my existence. I might be prepared, in my liberalism, to grant that such a response to the text might not be a rejection of faith. But saying that, I know that the ghost of Anti-Climacus is lurking somewhere to convince me that such a response is merely a different form of the offense. Indirect communication, in a text like this, must lead us not to unthinkable concepts or to proofs but to the decision of faith.

9

LIDENSKAB IN EFTERSKRIFT

A. H. Khan

In his attempt to define what it is to become a Christian Kierkegaard drew heavily on certain concepts some of which, he believed, had been conveniently forgotten by his contemporaries, made mere pleasantries in idle conversation, or held in contempt by the philosophy then fashionable in Denmark. One of these discredited concepts was Lidenskab or passion, a notion central to his pseudonymous work Afsluttende uvidenskabelig Efterskrift (Concluding Unscientific Postscript). In fact, this concept is central to the intent of its pseudonymous author Climacus and underlies all the themes he treats and the points he advances.

My main aim in this paper is to present a clear view of Climacus' understanding of the concept Lidenskab in Efterskrift. My purpose here is not so much to reach definite conclusions about this concept but, more importantly, to acquire an understanding of this concept, to discover precisely how Climacus treats it in this particular text. This is achieved by a description of some of the dominant relations among those terms which constitute the verbal environment of this concept and which therefore provide important clues to its outstanding features. Such an approach is neither novel nor new. In fact, it accords with the currently accepted view that a concept by itself has no more meaning than a mathematical point by itself has significance. Indeed, one gains a firm philosophical grasp of a concept precisely by becoming familiar with those features which are represented by the various significant relations among its associated terms.

In order to provide an accurate and detailed description of the various relations integral to a concept it is first necessary to identify objectively and systematically the terms associated with it. For this purpose I adopt a computer based method devised and reported by Alastair McKinnon.[1] The second and equally important aim of this paper is to put this method to a test to determine its reliability and accuracy. Of course, such a test requires that the concept selected be sufficiently known, or at least knowable, to permit others to evaluate the results easily and accurately. The concept Lidenskab, I believe, meets these requirements. It plays an important role in Efterskrift.[2] The word 'Lidenskab' occurs frequently enough to justify the use of such a method. Finally, as those who are familiar with Efterskrift intuitively know, the meaning of this concept in this text is sufficiently different from its ordinarily accepted one to be worthy of careful study.

The method has two distinct phases each with its own goal and each culminating in a different representation of the relations between Lidenskab and its associated terms. It would be wasted labour to describe each phase in detail as this has already been done elsewhere.[3] Instead, I shall give the briefest possible description of the steps taken in each phase to achieve these different goals.

The aim of the first phase is to identify those terms showing a marked tendency to co-occur with the search term and to arrange them in a table beginning with those most strongly tied to it. The steps taken to achieve this aim are the following:

1. Extract from the machine readable version of Efterskrift all sentences containing the search term, i.e., 'Lidenskab' and its definite form 'Lidenskaben', hereafter referred to as Lidenskab(1). Combine these sentences to form a synthetic or mini-text.
2. Produce a word frequency list showing the relative frequency of each word-type in this mini-text and in Kierkegaard's Samlede Værker.
3. Arrange the words in the frequency list beginning with those having the highest association index at the top of the list. This index is the ratio of the relative frequency

of the word in the mini-text to its relative frequency in the Samlede Værker.

4. Show in table 1 each of these top 40 words together with its association index and relative frequencies in the mini-text and the Samlede Værker or corpus, respectively.

These steps, of course, involve a number of choices which are obviously in need of at least minimal justification. The choice of the sentence as the co-occurrence unit was made on the assumption that the bearer of a complete thought in any literate work is the sentence and, further, that words associated with one another in a text tend to co-occur within a sentence. The choice concerning the number of variant forms to include in the search term was based on the importance and number of occurrences of each such form in the text. Both the main and definite forms of Lidenskab are clearly important and, as these occur 212 and 20 times respectively, their selection is obviously justifiable. However, this is not so clearly true of the other variant forms which together occur only 49 times, and which appear to be less semantically important and to have different and even inconsistent 'logics.' Finally, the top 40 words mentioned in step 4 were chosen on the basis of their association indices, which decreased quite rapidly after the 6.81 level. In fact, 32 of the top 40 words show comparatively high association indices ranging from 88.52 to 10.01. By contrast, those below the 6.77 level tend to be more weakly associated with our search term, less intuitively interesting, and often foreshadowed in the words already selected.

It is possible to deduce a good deal about our concept simply from the list of the top 40 words or terms associated with Lidenskab(1) and shown in table 1. This list shows 24 nouns, 13 modifiers and 3 verbs. It follows that this list of associated terms contains many more nouns than modifiers, a fact which, interestingly, supports a recently advanced hypothesis that nouns are primarily associated with other nouns.[4] This point aside, however, the following six nouns show comparatively high relative frequencies in our mini-text: Salighed, Troen, Existerende, Uendelighedens, Inderlighedens, and Existents. Further, five of the terms appear in this list in one or more variant forms. These include Comiske, Paradox, Subjektivitet, interesserede, and objektiv. Taken together these 11 allegedly tell-tale terms remind us that, if passion is eliminated, faith (Troen) no longer exists, that passion is intensified by holding on to the paradox (Paradox), that without passion it is impossible to be an existing person (Existerende) or to think about existing in existence (Existents), that the passion of the infinite (Uendelighedens) constitutes inwardness, that the corresponding passion of inwardness (Inderlighedens) is faith (Troen), and that a subject lacking an infinitely (uendeligt) passionate interest (interesserede) and basing his eternal happiness (Salighed) on objective (objektiv) inquiry expresses the comic (Comiske). It is possible to continue in this way connecting the remaining terms in this list and deducing more about the concept. But this can be done more accurately and quickly after the relation of these terms has been expressed spatially.

The aim of the second phase is to make available just such an array. This objective is reached by taking the following steps:

1. Construct a co-occurrence matrix showing the number of times each associated term co-occurs with every other such term in the various sentences of the mini-text. This gives the number of such co-occurrences in absolute numbers and is therefore designated as a raw co-occurrence matrix.
2. Correct this matrix by taking the absolute number of co-occurrences for each pair of associated terms and dividing it by the square root of the product of the number of their occurrences and multiplying the results by a suitable constant to give manageable values. This corrected co-occurrence matrix is shown in table 2.
3. Use the corrected values shown in table 2 as input to the KYST multidimensional scaling program to produce a three dimensional model of the various relations among the 40 associated terms. This model is shown in figure 1 and its ordinates in table 3.

The purpose of the second phase is to obtain the best possible spatial representation of the underlying relations among all the associated terms as these exist in all sentences of Efterskrift containing our search term. The first step gives an absolute but rough measure of the extent of the association between each pair of terms. The second step corrects these measures to yield a more accurate value, at the same time taking into account the extent to which the association between any given pair of terms might be due to chance. The third step produces an overall picture of all associations taking account of all of these at one and the same time. Comparison with the corrected co-occurrence matrix shows that the resulting model represents a very good approximation to the original data and this is confirmed by the fact that it shows a stress level of only 0.1297 on formula 1 of the KYST program.

So far we have followed McKinnon's procedure for retrieving those parts of Efterskrift containing the search term and for constructing a corresponding word list, matrix, and three-dimensional model of terms strongly associated with Lidenskab(1). His procedure also includes basic rules for the interpretation of a two dimensional model or map which are, however, equally applicable to a three dimensional one and are therefore cited here.

One rule is that terms near the centre of the model are associated with a large number of other terms in the set while those on its outer limits tend to be associated with a small number of these terms. This is obviously true of Lidenskab, evige, Salighed, and Existerende which are very close to the centre and are associated with 39, 32, 29, and 25 terms, respectively. It is also true of Vished, Bestemthed, Tænker, Pathos, and Dialektiske which lie on the periphery and are associated with 7, 8, 9, 10, and 10 terms, respectively. This kind of information can be quite useful in tracing those various connections of a term which play such an important role in defining the corresponding concept. It is not surprising that Salighed and Existerende are connected with many other terms for, like Lidenskab, they bear directly on the primary question of Efterskrift, viz., how is one to participate in the eternal (evige) happiness (Salighed) promised by Christianity? Climacus' answer is that one must have passion (Lidenskab) in order to be an existing individual (Existerende). Thus one can see at a glance the extent to which any term is associated with the other members of the set and hence the degree to which it is central to the understanding of the concept in question.

Another of McKinnon's rules is that terms clustering tightly together are associated either directly or indirectly with one another. However, this rule does not appear immediately relevant since our model shows no such tightly knit clusters; indeed, it seems best regarded as one large overall cluster. In this connection it is nevertheless relevant to point out that the search term is presumed to lie at the centre of our model and that the distance between it and its associated terms does not therefore accurately reflect the strength of their (direct) tie or association. Equally important, the distance between pairs of terms is a function of their corrected co-occurrence value and the corresponding value which each has with every other term in the set. Consequently a particular pair may be closely situated without being particularly closely tied (according to the matrix) or be far apart without having a particularly low corrected co-occurrence score. Doubts on such matters can be resolved by checking the relevant values in the corrected co-occurrence matrix, though, one must add, the model affords an overall view while the matrix of course does not. Put another way, the model shows not the strength of the ties between terms in the set as such but rather the overall relations among the various terms as these occur in the synthetic text organized around the search term.

Given such a model, many connections can be easily seen. Indeed, those between the following eight pairs are so obvious that they do not require any comment: evige and Salighed, uendelig and interesseret, uendelig and interesserede, Dialektiske and Modsigelsen, Paradox and Troen, objektive and Uvished, existerende and Subjekt, and Subjektivitet and Inderlighed. Other such pairs suggested by our model and matrix are the following: Bestemthed and Subjektiv, absolut and Inderlighed, and Tænker and Existents. The connections and significance of these eleven pairs, as well as those of others not mentioned but clearly suggested by the model, have been carefully investigated.

On the basis of that investigation I submit the following brief report which incorporates all the associated terms in the model, preserves as much as possible of the original sentences containing these terms, and, we believe, brings out or underscores the main points of this concept.

One of Climacus' main points about passion is that it is a decisive factor for a genuinely human existence. No one, he tells us, can even think about existing (existerende) while in existence (Existents) because to exist (existere) involves a contradiction (Modsigelsen) which a truly subjective (subjektive) thinker (Tænker) lives with. If he were to abandon or fail to notice the contradiction, he would be without passion (Lidenskab), and his thinking about genuinely existing would be tantamount to his forgetting that he is himself already existing (Existerende).[5]

A second and closely related point is that without passion there can be no concern for an eternal happiness. The "question of one's eternal (evige) happiness (Salighed)," Climacus tells us, does not arise "except for the infinitely (unendeligt) interested (interesserede) subject in passion (Lidenskab)."[6] This question cannot be treated objectively any more than the question of one's immortality can be so treated. Whoever seeks the determinateness (Bestemthed) of immortality is far removed from being subjective (subjektiv), for he has allowed his subjectivity (Subjectivitet) to become indefinite instead of intensifying his passion to embrace (forholde) the indeterminateness of immortality.[7]

Treating the question of one's eternal happiness objectively (objectivt) does not generate the infinitely (uendeligt) interested (interesseret) passion (Lidenskab) which is necessary to embrace such happiness.[8] Whatever passion might be generated through or connected with such a treatment does not differ in any significant way from that which the historian exhibits in his quest to reach absolute (absolut) certainty (Vished) from his study of historical documents. Of course, as historian his passion (Lidenskab) is at the most objective (objective) and not subjective (subjektive), and hence he is not in contradiction with himself.[9]

A third point concerning objectivity provides a deeper understanding of Climacus' rejection of any objective or even speculative approach to the question of one's eternal happiness. This point is best stated as follows: any kind of objective (objectiv) approach simply eliminates that infinite (uendelige) passion (Lidenskab) which is necessary for concern with one's eternal (evige) happiness (Salighed) to take root. The reason is that the result (Resultat) of an objective (objektiv) approach does not permit the admission of any contradiction, not even that inherent in dealing objectively with one's own eternal happiness. In fact, the contradiction is that learned inquiry insists upon certainty but at the most can produce only an approximate result when dealing with such happiness. Owing to its quest for an absolute certainty it cannot acknowledge any contradiction.[10] Should an infinitely (uendeligt) concerned subject (Subjekt) who is not naturally comical (comisk) try to base his eternal (evige) happiness (Salighed) on any objective result, he would simply express the comic (Comiske).[11]

A fourth and important point is that passion becomes dialectical in character when and only when it is at its very maximum. An absolute requirement for being related to one's eternal happiness, this heightened passion is referred to as subjectivity (Subjektivitet) or (Inderlighed).[12] In fact Climacus holds that a secret inwardness (Inderlighed) in absolute (absolut) passion (Lidenskab) is the mark of being truly human.[13] Characterizing this inwardness, however, is a pathos (Pathos) which is immediate, but is unlike other kinds of immediate pathos in having a dialectical factor (Dialektiske). This factor excites passion (Lidenskaben) to its highest pitch, thereby giving tension to the contradiction (Modsigelsen) and deepening the inwardness for becoming related (forholde) to an eternal happiness.[14]

Objectively (objektivt) understood, the infinite (uendelige) passion (Lidenskab) of inwardness (Inderlighedens) is really required for the uncertainty which makes the contradiction possible. When this objective (objectiv) uncertainty (Uvished) is embraced with the entire passion of the infinite (Uendelighedens), inwardness (Inderlighed) increases and subjectivity (Subjektiviteten) becomes a truth within the person.[15] This truth is the paradox (Paradoxet) only when it is held fast with the entire passion (Lidenskaben) of inwardness (Inderlighedens), and it ceases to be such when passion (Lidenskaben) is lacking and the person forgets that he is an existing (existerende) subject (Subjekt).[16] Put another way, without passion there is no paradox, and vice versa. To quote Climacus, "Subjectivity (Subjektiviteten) culminates in passion, Christianity is the paradox (Paradoxet), paradox (Paradox) and passion (Lidenskab) are a mutual fit . . . ."[17]

A fifth and final point links passion, paradox, and faith together. The passion of inwardness (Inderlighedens) occasioned by holding on to the paradox (Paradoxet) as long as one exists is designated as faith (Troen). Without faith no such passion can be maintained or, for that matter, discovered in the first place.[18] The infinite (uendelige) personal interestedness in passion is in one instance the potentiality of faith (Troens) and in the next faith (Troen) itself; in one instance the form of an eternal happiness, and in the next eternal (evige) happiness (Salighed) itself.[19] Hence passion is not just a condition of faith but, fitted with the paradox, is faith itself.

The preceding five points summarize only the dominant

relations between the terms associated with our concept. A longer report might well provide a more detailed description of these relations but, we stress, these points do not exhaust all that can be said about this concept. They do, however, bring out its cardinal features and thus provide an important contribution to the understanding of the concept of passion in Kierkegaard's corpus. They are also a reminder of a certain lack of clarity in this concept, e.g., whether subjectivity, inwardness, and faith are to be understood as modalities of a particular passion, or simply as different names for a specific passion. In this sense they direct attention to familiar relations which are presumably clear but which in fact are not, to things we need to notice but have never needed to notice before. They remind us of the familiar and distinctive features of the concept, features present in the mind but never always present to the mind as facts, features sometimes hidden from us only because of their familiarity and simplicity.[20] Not to heed these points is undoubtedly to miss noticing features of this concept worth noticing and, consequently, to fail to acquire even a rudimentary understanding of it.

By way of summary I recall the features already described. Passion is a selective capacity for the highest possible involvement. It is suited to just one object which is infinite, absolute, personal and applicable to every person, namely one's eternal happiness. It is immediate but is marked off from other kinds of immediacy and further defined by a dialectical factor which excites it to its highest pitch and which, in effect, is the objective uncertainty of one's eternal happiness. At its highest pitch, this passion is faith, which in turn is the deepest level of inwardness, subjectivity, or human existence. By virtue of its unique object, it is both a personal involvement and a capacity. But it is selective for, even though present to itself, it may not be manifested until it is deliberately and consciously activated.

I conclude by reminding you of the two aims of this paper. The primary aim is to present a clear view of Climacus' understanding of the concept. The secondary aim is to evaluate the reliability and accuracy of a computer based method for investigating concepts. The first has been accomplished through the report and the preceding summary paragraphs, and has been achieved by following closely the steps in the two phases of the method and by basing the report primarily upon its final output. Whatever doubts there may have been about the reliability of the word list and the accuracy of the relations represented in the model were dispelled by a detailed study of the relations between the various key associated terms within the mini-text. The accuracy and detail of the account of the concept offered in this paper is clear evidence that the method works effectively—— at least I am so persuaded. I conclude, however, on a more Kierkegaardian note: "Judge for yourselves!"

Table 1. Words most closely associated with 'Lidenskab' in Efterskrift

Word	Translation/ Use	Association Index	Relative Frequency Mini-Text	Relative Frequency Corpus
interesserede	interested	88.52	11.40	0.13
Lidenskab	passion	76.47	258.29	3.38
interesseret	interested	64.15	15.19	0.24
Lidenskaben	passion	61.47	22.79	0.37
Uendelighedens	of the infinite	40.98	24.06	0.59
Subjektivitet	subjectivity	40.03	8.86	0.22
Inderlighedens	of inwardness	33.63	20.26	0.60
subjektiv	subjective	32.48	8.86	0.27
Subjekt	subject	30.32	11.40	0.38
objektiv	objective	29.60	16.46	0.56
objektivt	objectively	27.32	12.66	0.46
subjektive	subjective	25.88	12.66	0.49
objektive	objective	23.20	12.66	0.55
Uvished	uncertainty	22.95	8.86	0.39
Modsigelsen	contradiction	19.14	16.46	0.86
Subjektiviteten	subjectivity	18.38	10.13	0.55
Existerende	exister	17.95	25.32	1.41
Dialektiske	dialectical	17.74	8.86	0.50
Bestemthed	determinateness	16.71	8.86	0.53
uendeligt	infinitely	13.66	22.79	1.67
Pathos	pathos	13.59	12.66	0.93
comisk	comical	13.26	25.32	1.91
Paradox	paradox	13.14	8.86	0.67
Salighed	happiness	12.92	39.25	3.04
evige	eternal	12.74	29.12	2.29
existerende	existing	11.54	16.46	1.43
Resultat	result	11.40	8.86	0.78
Paradoxet	paradox	10.69	13.93	1.30
forholde	embrace	10.69	11.40	1.07
uendelige	infinite	10.13	27.86	2.75
Tænker	thinker	10.01	8.86	0.89
existere	to exist	9.49	13.93	1.47
Vished	certainty	9.41	8.86	0.94
Existents	of existence	8.92	20.26	2.27
Troens	of faith	8.88	16.46	1.85
Inderlighed	inwardness	8.82	18.99	2.15
Comiske	comic	7.48	11.40	1.52
absolut	absolute	6.81	20.26	2.98
Troen	faith	6.78	27.86	4.11

	Freq.	absolut	Bestemthed	comisk	Comiske	Dialektiske	evige	Existents	existere	Existerende	existerende	forholde	Inderlighed	Inderlighedens	interesserede	interesseret	Lidenskab	Lidenskaben	Modsigelsen	objektiv	objective
absolut	16																				
Bestemthed	7																				
comisk	20																				
Comiske	9			52.2																	
Dialektiske	7	9.5																			
evige	23	10.4		28.0	13.9	15.8															
Existents	16	6.3	56.7			9.5	5.2														
existere	11	15.1				22.8		37.7													
Existerende	20	5.6	101.4			8.5	9.3	55.9	20.2												
existerende	13	6.9	63.0					34.7	16.7	37.2											
forholde	9	16.7	75.7			37.8	20.9	16.7		22.4	18.5										
Inderlighed	15	45.2		11.5			16.2			23.1											
Inderlighedens	16			5.6			5.2			5.6	13.9		12.9								
interesserede	9			22.4	11.1		34.8														
interesseret	12			51.6	28.9		48.2					9.6	14.9								
Lidenskab	204	28.0	18.5	34.4	23.3	13.2	36.5	35.0	23.2	34.4	25.2	16.3	32.5	31.5	25.7	28.3					
Lidenskaben	18	11.8				35.7	9.8		14.2	5.3	19.6	23.6			7.9		6.6				
Modsigelsen	13	6.9				42.0	17.4		33.5	12.4				6.9	9.3		23.3	13.1			
objektiv	13			12.4		10.5	34.7							6.9	9.3	8.0	27.1	6.5			
objektive	10						6.6			7.1	17.5			55.4			26.6		8.8		
objektivt	10	7.9					6.6		19.1	7.1		10.5		15.8		9.1	24.4	22.4	17.5		10.0
Paradox	7	18.9					7.9			16.9	31.5			18.9			23.8	8.9			12.0
Paradoxet	11	15.1		6.7						6.7	16.7			37.7			31.7				9.5
Pathos	10					35.9	13.2				8.8	42.2	8.2				15.5	22.4			
Resultat	7						55.2						9.8		25.2		18.5	17.8	63.0		
Salighed	31	22.5		28.1	18.0	20.4	97.4	4.5		4.0		29.9	9.3		47.9	41.5	40.2	12.7	19.9	54.8	
Subjekt	9						7.0				64.8			16.7	11.1	38.5	18.7	23.6	9.3		
subjektiv	7		171.4				7.9	18.9		50.7	31.5	25.2				10.9	23.8		10.5	10.5	12.0
subjektive	10						6.6	7.9	28.6	14.1	26.3			7.9			31.0		17.5	8.8	10.0
Subjektivitet	7	9.5	85.7	16.9	12.6		39.4	9.5		16.9	10.5	12.6	39.1		25.2	21.8	23.8			31.5	
Subjektiviteten	8						14.7								23.6		32.2	16.7			
Troen	22	37.3					13.3							26.7			23.9	35.2	5.9		13.5
Troens	13	20.8					17.4	6.9		18.6			14.3				25.2		7.7		
Tænker	7				25.2			28.4	11.4	16.9	10.5						23.8				
uendelig	22		48.4	23.8	14.2		31.1	5.3		14.3	17.7	7.1	22.0		7.1	61.6	37.3		23.7		6.7
uendelige	13						17.4			6.2				20.8			31.1		7.7	23.1	8.8
Uendelighedens	19							5.7		15.4			11.8	5.7			35.3				14.5
uendeligt	18			31.6	7.9		39.3	5.9				7.9	12.2		70.8	34.0	34.7	5.6	6.5	32.7	
Uvished	7													56.7			18.5		10.5		107.7
Vished	7	28.4					7.9										31.8	8.9		10.5	12.0

	Freq.	objektivt	Paradox	Paradoxet	Pathos	Resultat	Salighed	Subjekt	subjektiv	subjektive	Subjektivitet	Subjektiviteten	Troen	Troens	Tænker	uendelig	uendelige	Uendelighedens	uendeligt	Uvished
Paradox	7																			
Paradoxet	11		57.0																	
Pathos	10																			
Resultat	7	35.9			12.0															
Salighed	31	5.7			22.7	40.7														
Subjekt	9		50.4	20.1			6.0													
subjektiv	7						6.8													
subjektive	10						5.7													
Subjektivitet	7						54.3		28.6											
Subjektiviteten	8	11.2	13.4	21.3		26.7	12.7													
Troen	22	6.7	16.1	32.2		8.1	7.7	7.1												
Troens	13		10.5	8.4		10.5	10.0						53.2							
Tænker	7								14.3	23.9				21.0						
uendelig	22	13.5			6.7	32.3	30.6	7.1	16.1	6.7	24.2									
uendelige	13	17.5				10.5	19.9					19.6	17.7	15.4		5.9				
Uendelighedens	19	14.5								7.3		16.2		6.4			12.7			
uendeligt	18	7.5				17.8	50.8	15.7	8.9		26.7	16.7				5.0				
Uvished	7	12.0		11.4									16.1				10.5	17.3		
Vished	7	12.0					13.6		14.3				8.1					8.7	8.9	

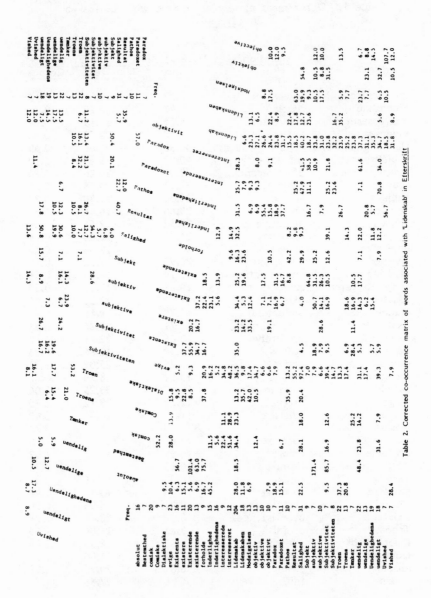

Table 2. Corrected co-occurrence matrix of words associated with 'Lidenskab' in Efterskrift

Table 3. Coordinates of three dimensional model

Word	x	y	z
absolut	0.347	0.293	0.151
Bestemthed	-1.126	0.445	-0.340
comisk	-0.162	-0.970	-0.700
Comiske	-0.742	-0.581	-0.971
Dialektiske	-0.527	0.319	1.016
evige	-0.146	-0.334	0.092
existents	-0.655	0.784	0.019
existere	-0.326	1.103	0.553
Existerende	-0.225	0.562	-0.106
existerende	-0.176	0.505	-0.392
forholde	-0.933	0.268	0.449
Inderlighed	-0.142	-0.025	-0.623
Inderlighedens	0.883	-0.040	-0.382
interesserede	-0.294	-1.118	0.314
interesseret	-0.580	-0.855	-0.326
Lidenskab	0.030	-0.007	-0.112
Lidenskaben	0.085	0.018	0.920
Modsigelsen	-0.017	0.304	0.518
objektiv	0.033	-0.653	0.231
objektive	0.578	0.250	-0.731
objektivt	0.397	-0.067	0.605
Paradox	0.981	0.397	0.012
Paradoxet	1.015	-0.217	-0.578
Pathos	-1.004	-0.016	0.726
Resultat	-0.015	-0.463	0.843
Salighed	-0.339	-0.354	0.266
Subjekt	0.328	-0.420	-0.463
subjektiv	-0.754	0.165	-0.643
subjektive	0.149	0.990	-0.233
Subjektivitet	-1.001	-0.319	-0.158
Subjektiviteten	0.794	-0.817	0.407
Troen	0.925	0.119	0.548
Troens	0.466	0.781	0.357
Tænker	-0.523	1.090	-0.805
uendelig	-0.528	-0.148	-0.206
uendelige	0.846	-0.336	0.297
Uendelighedens	0.806	0.679	-0.433
uendeligt	-0.544	-0.731	0.233
Uvished	1.555	0.194	-0.089
Vished	0.542	-0.795	-0.258

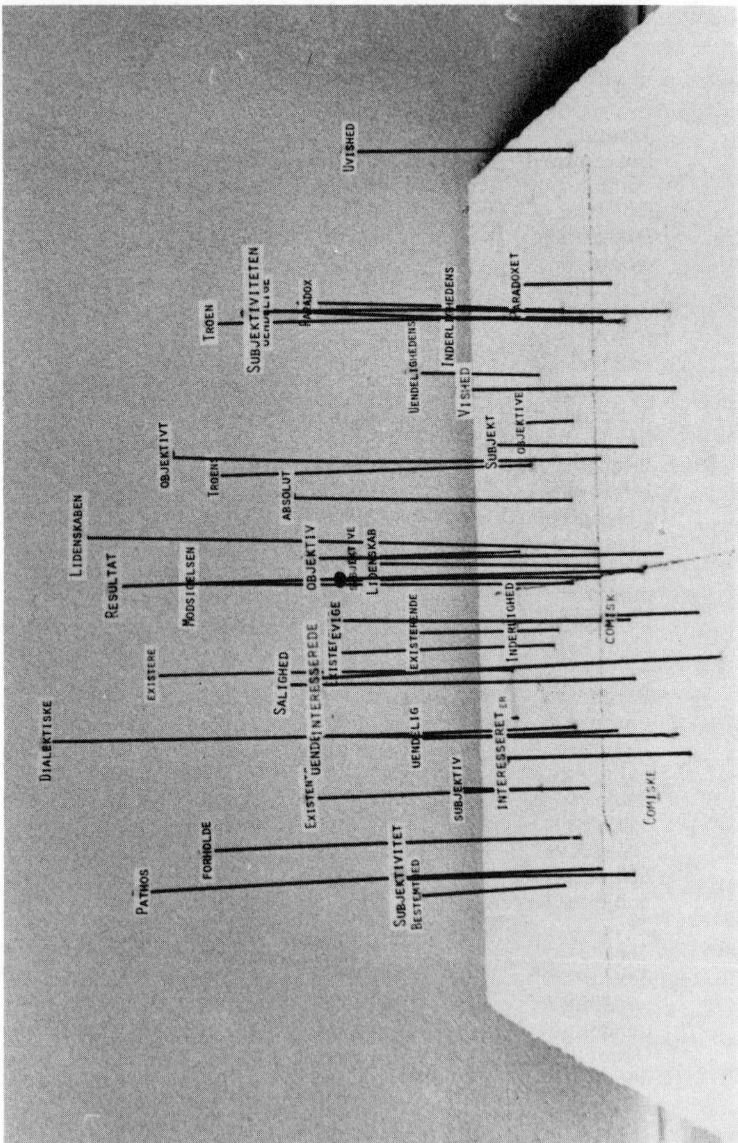

Figure 1. Model of topography of 'Lidenskab' in <u>Efterskrift</u>

Comment on Khan

David Goicoechea

The computer method can be of great aid to research because of its thoroughness and exactness. If someone is working on a project such as "Passion in the Postscript" it might reveal unnoticed relations between terms. Thus, the scholar can use it as a check on himself so that he does not make the mistake of missing the obvious.

However, certain cautions are in order. Perhaps the first is one which Kierkegaard himself made. He distinguished between quantitative accumulation and the qualitative leap. He argued that the quantity of evidence did not suffice for the subjective decision. The latter could be made only by a qualitative leap. This distinction also indicates the limitations of the computer method. The number of times that certain terms appear in the same sentence does indicate the degree of their interrelatedness. However, certain terms may be very importantly interrelated and this may not be indicated by their frequent textual juxtaposition. This might occur especially in Kierkegaard because of his method of indirect communication. As he tries to communicate to the deep structures of a person he might write very much about certain ideas. And at the same time he might mention a key idea very seldom. He seems to think that effective pedagogy can make meaningful an important idea by emphasizing it through secretiveness and almost in silence. Thus, the silence of Abraham and the last word of Socrates get a person to sit up and take notice in a way that pedantic verbosity does not. The computer method would fail to detect a term of great importance used indirectly and only a time or two. The qualitative importance of a term is not always in direct proportion to its quantitative usage. An example of such a phenomenon concerning "Passion in the Postscript" is "truth." For it is not mentioned that often in the Postscript, and yet it is a key term in both the Fragments and the Postscript where Kierkegaard is moving away from "the philosophical." His new definition of "truth"—"objective uncertainty held fast in the appropriation process of passionate inwardness"— stands out as one of the landmarks of existential thought. And yet the computer cannot detect this even though "truth" here is intimately related to "passion."

Also, the computer method has the danger of promoting mere observation and thus demoting philosophical analysis. Dr. Khan's paper presents the groundwork for a philosophical paper but it is not yet a philosophical paper. He links together a series of related terms which the computer dictates. But he does not go beyond concatenation to conceptual analysis. Philosophically he needs to show how and why "passion" is related to "truth," for example. But the computer method does not detect "truth" and distracts him to many related issues before he takes the time to think existentially. It is valuable to see that "passion" is related to so many terms. But what is passion and how is it related? This the computer cannot say and Dr. Khan does not say. The philosopher needs to define and distinguish key terms to build up a demonstration for a thesis. By becoming involved in the great counting project one could forget this.

We might make this point in one more way by asking a question. What is the relation between such terms as "passion," "faith," "existence," "eternal happiness," etc.? Are they used univocally or analogously? Are they related as identical or as different but co-constitutive? Dr. Khan seems to see them as univocal and as identical. But assumptions based on quantificational co-occurrence blur the very distinctions that make up philosophical inquiry. Are the assumptions justified? If the terms are analogous, in what way is this so? Is it through analogy of proportion or attribution? Or does Kierkegaard develop a new type of existential analogy? Plato would deal with such issues concerning the forms, and Aquinas concerning the attributes of God, and Heidegger concerning the existentialia of Dasein. Does Kierkegaard fail in such philosophical precision? Or did he develop a new existential dialectic which was just as careful about such distinctions? Would not his whole project be aimed at distinguishing the passion of Hegel, Socrates, and Jesus? And thus would there not be a special existential network for Hegel, and a special one for Socrates, and a special one for the Christian thinker? And must not the computer fail to see the very point of the Kierkegaardian analysis? Does it not necessarily see "passion" as a univocal term? Does it not necessarily tend to equate "Passion" and "Faith" etc.?

But these criticisms are only cautions. If the computer project is used in the Kierkegaardian spirit of moving toward the religious by way of the aesthetic, then it can be of great value. It can exemplify Kierkegaard's pedagogic principle of "deceiving into the truth." It can meet the people of our time in order to get them to sit up and take notice of the eternal. Just as St. Paul could say that he was making up in his sufferings for what was lacking in the sufferings of Christ, so we might say that McKinnon and Khan are making up in the passion of their labour for what was lacking in the passion of Kierkegaard.

10

THE SHAPE OF KIERKEGAARD'S AUTHORSHIP

Alastair McKinnon

Kierkegaard spent much time and energy planning and reflecting on his authorship and, as the Papirer show, gave much thought to the relation of its various parts to one another. More recently, certain commentators have been concerned with this latter problem while other less serious scholars appear to identify Kierkegaard with but one part of his authorship or, as one sometimes suspects, even with a particular book. In this study I try to question such approaches by attempting to place the various works in their proper relation to one another and to the authorship as a whole. I do so with the aid of a three-dimensional model, and in this sense at least my title is to be taken quite literally.

As some of you may know, I have already done a number of such studies on a variety of bases and, indeed, hope to do more. These include pronouns, proper names, the hundred most frequent words in the corpus, punctuation, sentence and word length, and an earlier study published in an obscure journal using what I call aberrant frequency or ABFREQ words.[1] The present study is also based on such words but employs a slightly revised formula for determining whether a word shows aberrant frequency in a particular book and certain other minor modifications as well. If I appear to be repeating already published work this is not because I wish to escape the burden of producing a new paper but because these words appear to be the most promising basis for clustering the works and because I seek your comments and criticisms before proceeding further.

The method consists of three distinct and perhaps not altogether simple steps which are as follows:

1. Identify and list all words in each book whose frequency in that book is aberrant, i.e., represents $|S.D.| => 2.58$ from the corpus norm.
2. Discover the percentage of aberrant frequency (ABFREQ) words common to each pair of books, matching "+'s" with "+'s" and "-'s" with "-'s", using the following formula:

$$\frac{c}{A + B - c} \times 100$$

where A = the number of ABFREQ words in book A
B = the number of ABFREQ words in book B
c = the number of ABFREQ words common to books A and B.

3. Using these percentages as similarity indices, input these values into the KYST multi-dimensional scaling program[2] to produce a three dimensional model of optimal fit.

I should perhaps add that there is also the fourth step of building the model using the three-dimensional coordinates produced by the program and with some help from the three two-dimensional representations it provides.

I have already described the first of these steps in a recently published rather technical paper[3] and hope before long to provide another more detailed account set within the context of the larger issues of text interpretation. For the moment I shall therefore provide only the briefest and sketchiest description of the central concept underlying this approach.

Though we often think of an author's vocabulary simply in terms of the words which he uses, it is obvious that we ought also to consider the frequency with which he uses these words and, in the present case, their frequency in a particular book in relation to their frequency in Kierkegaard's corpus as a whole. It is further evident that an author writes each book on a particular subject, in a given style, for a specific audience, within a certain literary tradition, etc., and will therefore almost certainly use some words much more frequently and others much less frequently than is his normal custom. Such departures can be measured in a number of ways, including the number of standard deviations represented by the frequency of a word in a particular book from its corpus norm or average. The critical points in such deviations are usually assumed to be |=>1.96|, |=>2.58|, |=>3.89|, etc. but about this more later. For the moment it is sufficient to say that we shall employ the second of these values and that there is therefore never more than a 1% chance that any of our selected words are not truly aberrant and, in the vast majority of cases, a very much smaller chance that this is not so. Briefly, the frequency of virtually all such words requires explanation. Put another way, almost every one of these words may be regarded as significant and characteristic features of the work in question.

Of course, comparative vocabulary studies are by no means new. What distinguishes the present one is the fact that it concentrates upon those vocabulary items which are clearly and demonstrably characteristic features of the works in question and neglects all those words which, from the point of view of such studies, are, to use the current jargon, "noise."

The concept of aberrant frequency is illustrated in figure 1 which shows the number of standard deviations of Du in all the works of Kierkegaard's corpus. The solid line represents the corpus norm or relative frequency of this word which is 0.004488 or, multiplying by 10,000 to get a more convenient and readily intelligible value, 44.88. The dotted lines represent +1.96 and -1.96 and the broken lines +2.58 and -2.58 standard deviations from this norm. The number of such deviations for this word in each of the books is represented by the dot immediately above its title code. Thus we can immediately see that Du has an aberrantly high frequency in CT and TS and an aberrantly low frequency in SV and AE. Briefly, I hold that the statistically significant excess frequency of Du in the first two of these books is an important characteristic which they share and that the similarly significant deficient frequency of this word in the last two books is also one of their very many such readily identifiable and characteristic features. This study is based upon the assumption that the number or, better, the percentage of such aberrant frequency words which two works have in common is a very accurate and percipient measure of their similarity.

A moment ago I spoke of aberrant frequency words as

those whose frequency in a given book was such as to require explanation. In most cases that explanation will be due to the content and style of the work in question but in certain cases it might possibly be due primarily to the author's current literary habits. I shall not attempt to describe here all the research and experimentation we have done in order to discover the best possible cut-off point for the exclusion of most such words but will simply report that, after much investigation, we decided upon the value of |=> 2.58|. This decision perhaps involves a loss of a relatively small number of possibly important and characteristic words but, as will be seen, it leaves very, very large numbers of such words whose status is not in any possible doubt.

Our ABFREQ2 program generates lists of all ABFREQ words for each of our 34 works. Table 1 shows the number of tokens, types, aberrant frequency words (|S.D.|=>2.58) and these aberrant frequency words as a percentage of all word types in each of these books. Note that the number of such ABFREQ words varies from 280 for EOT to 2,751 for BI and their percentage from 11.11 for SV to 37.29 for LP. Note further that the total number of aberrant frequency word types for all these works is 39,233.

Those in doubt concerning the justification of this part of our approach are invited to examine the aberrant frequency word lists for a number of Kierkegaard's more familiar works shown in tables 2a-2d. Note that in all cases these lists of words are arranged in descending order according to their number of standard deviations, that the cut-off point is not always the same, and that even in these very high values there are some negative standard deviations. Note too the extent to which these words represent important features of the works in question.

As already indicated, the second step is to have the computer match the aberrant frequency word lists for every pair of works, assigning a score of one for every word which appears as either aberrantly high or aberrantly low in both works but, of course, not doing so for those which are aberrantly high in one and aberrantly low in the other. The result of this operation is shown in table 3a which gives the absolute number of ABFREQ words common to each pair of books in the corpus. This is interesting information but its usefulness is vitiated to some extent by the very great difference in size between the various works. Accordingly, we use the formula already indicated to calculate the percentage which these common ABFREQ words represent of all ABFREQ words in both books. This value shows the percentage of distinguishing characteristic words or features in each book which are common to both and so provides an accurate, reliable, overall similarity index. All these values are shown in table 3b and range from 0.14 for LA and TAF to 13.17 for OTA and CT.

I recognize that such a mass of data appears, at least at first glance, virtually indigestible. But I also recall Kierkegaard's remark that when one pursues the truth one need not be in a hurry. Accordingly, I suggest that before proceeding the reader consider an abstract or summary of these data in order to judge for himself whether these results are reliable.

The abstract given in table 3c shows the two books which, according to this approach, are most like and the two least like every other book in the corpus. For example, the first line shows that BI and EE1 are the two books most like and TAF and EOT the two books least like LP. So, too, for all the other works in the corpus. I trust that the reader will find these results convincing or at least in accord with his conceptions and that we may now proceed.

The third step in our method was to input all the similarity indices shown in table 3b into the KYST multidimensional scaling program in order that, by a series of very long and complex mathematical computations, it might calculate the optimum point for each of our 34 books within a three-dimensional space. The coordinates for these points are shown in table 4 and the spatial model based upon them in figure 2. The calculation of these points is an extremely difficult matter as may be inferred from the fact that our original data is actually of 33 dimensions. There are however a number of reasons to believe that the program has been successful. The relation of these points shows substantial agreement with the summary of our matrix shown in table 3c and, though this is a much more difficult matter to estimate, with the values of the original matrix shown in table 3b. Further, this configuration shows a stress of only 0.131 on formula 1 of the KYST program. We conclude therefore that this is a satisfactory representation of all the original data and add as our only qualification that it is of course only in three dimensions. That, however, is a concession to the human mind rather than to the computer which has none of our difficulties with four or more dimensions.

Before proceeding it may help to add some general remarks concerning the interpretation of such models. Briefly, they are genuinely "free space" models which can be rotated about any or all of their axes. Hence top and bottom, like left and right, are completely irrelevant. The present axes are simply convenient devices in terms of which to define the location of our points or works. Their essential explicit features are simply their various inter-point and centre-point distances. Note, however, that their point of origin does represent the centre of the corpus and that the works at the back of our model (i.e., those showing negative x coordinates) are apparently sufficiently more heterogeneous than those at the front that, to express the matter one way, they have driven the y axis to the fore of the model.

It is impossible to stress too strongly that the similarity indices shown in table 3b, the three dimensional coordinates in table 4, and, particularly, the model shown in figure 2 are the real and in some sense perhaps the only finally valid results of this study. Indeed, if I could give each of you a model I would do so and say nothing more. I realize, however, that you may find these results simply strange and perplexing and offer the following as an example of some of the conclusions which appear to be implied.

Note that most of the early pseudonymous works form a cluster with EE1, EE2, BA, SV, and AE at its core and G, FB, PS, and F on its periphery. Note too that BI appears to belong to this cluster, that LA and possibly even LP are perhaps on its periphery, but that the allegedly pseudonymous KK certainly is not.

The second most obvious cluster consists of the mainly early religious works T, TTL, OTA, KG, CT, and possibly even IC; certainly the latter shows strong ties with most of the other works in this cluster. (See, for example, the relevant similarity indices in table 3b.)

The next most obvious cluster is made up of the three later religious discourses YTS, TAF, and EOT with, perhaps, LF and, possibly, GU.

Continuing counter-clockwise, the next cluster consists of books all of which I should be tempted to describe as attack literature. These appear to include TS, DS, B21, Ø, and, perhaps, IC. I note here that I myself regard HCD as part of this literature but that our results show it to be an extreme outlyer. About this, perhaps more later.

The three meta-works in the corpus, viz., BFF, SFV, and FV, together form a very loose cluster. The last two deal with precisely the same subject and have a relatively high similarity index (7.05) but are nevertheless some distance apart in our model. In the circumstances, this must be due to the fact that FV shows relatively low scores with most of the rest of the corpus and may be some kind of support for those who, noting the absence of any manuscript in Kierkegaard's hand for this work, conjecture that it may have been written by someone else.

Some will no doubt find it strange that GU and HCD, the only two sermons in the corpus, are so distant from one another. In fact, or so I would argue, their differences far outweigh this formal similarity. GU is a pure case of religious and devotional discourse and HCD, I believe, another such case of the attack literature. It is, I suggest, a mark of the sophistication and percipience of our method that it identifies and indicates their differences so clearly.

Though I have not said so, it would seem that TSA might be regarded as part of the attack literature; certainly, though written before the attack, it helps to lay some of its theoretical foundations. In this connection note its relatively strong tie with IC (4.25) and, particularly, with Ø (3.07). The fact remains, however, that this piece does not appear to fit readily into any of the main groups of the corpus. For example, it shows significant ties with BA, PS, AE, KG, CT, SD, and SFV. It is therefore perhaps best seen as something of an outlyer which is of course what our model suggests. This is perhaps also true of KK which shows significant ties with such diverse works as EE1, EE2, BA, SV, AE, LA, CT, TSA, SD, IC, B21, but strong ties only with SFV (2.32) and BFF (2.27).

So much for these works and their relation to one another. The last column in table 4 shows the distance of each from the centroid or point of origin of our model. It is important to be quite clear about the significance of this column. It does not tell us which of Kierkegaard's works are most and which are least important but rather which are most and which least like the Samlede Værker as a whole. For example, it shows that GU and HCD are, at least on this method of reckoning, least typical while Ø and IC are most typical or representative of all his published works. Note that this tells heavily against the familiar thesis that Ø is the strange and eccentric product of an unfortunately disintegrating mind. I believe that Dr. Malantschuk would have rejoiced to see this confirmation of his own quite different estimate of this work.

Aristotle distinguishes between knowledge of the fact and knowledge of the reasoned fact. All our remarks thus far have been about how things are and the time has come to ask instead why they are as they are. In this connection it should help to look at some lists of ABFREQ words common to a number of different pairs of books. Severely abbreviated versions of four of these lists are shown in tables 5a-5d and, as an interesting contrast, that for GU and HCD in table 5e. Note that in each of these five cases the total number of such words is shown at the bottom of the list. Note also that these common words are arranged in approximately descending order according to the product of their standard deviations in the works in question. I trust that you will agree that the first four of these lists provide insight into the nature of the similarity between these pairs of works and that the fact that GU and HCD have only six ABFREQ words in common is itself evidence that they are not very similar.

I have been arguing that it is possible to produce a percipient and suggestive clustering of Kierkegaard's works by comparing aberrant frequency words and proceed now to ask whether one can use this same basis to identify and describe the real dimensions or lines of force (if there are such dimensions and lines) within Kierkegaard's work as a whole. In the current terminology of multidimensional scaling, I move now from cluster to dimensional analysis. I shall do so, however, only briefly and remind the reader that what follows is based in part upon choices and interpretations which are to some extent subjective and that he should not therefore regard any apparently mistaken conclusions in the following as reflecting upon the validity of our general approach.

The original version of this paper concluded with the remark that just before its delivery I had discovered a significant error in this part of the study. In fact, it now appears, I had made two distinct though related errors. The first was in focussing attention upon the clusters already identified and the second in concentrating upon those words showing aberrant frequency in each and every book within these clusters. In the present version I attempt to correct these errors by focussing instead upon slightly different groups of books and upon those words showing aberrant frequency for these groups as such. Though there is some element of choice in the selection of these new groups there is also an objective basis as indicated below.

In general, the real dimensions of such a model are meaningful and interpretable directions joining points or groups of points representing clearly different positions or attitudes in respect of some important issue or question. They can therefore be conceived as lines passing through its point of origin and joining diagonally opposite points or groups of points usually widely separated from each other. Even with these criteria it is perhaps not very easy to identify such axes from the picture of our model shown in figure 2, but it is not too difficult to do so from the model itself. Certainly it seems that the first real axis is that joining EE1, EE2, BA, PS, SV, and AE (hereafter group 1) to IC, Ø, DS, B21, and HCD (group 2) and that the second is that joining LP, LA, BFF, SFV, and FV (group 3) to T, TTL, OTA, KG, CT, LF, YTS, TAF, and GU (group 4). We now attempt to describe these lines or dimensions and thus articulate the underlying structure of Kierkegaard's authorship.

I pause here to spell out my aim by means of a now standard textbook example. In March 1968, Prof. Myron Wish asked 18 students in a psychology measurement course to rate the degree of overall similarity between 12 nations on a scale ranging from 1 to 9. The mean similarity ratings for each pair were then computed and put into the KYST multidimensional scaling program which in turn produced a two-dimensional array showing the relations of these nations as perceived by these students. In fact, all the countries in the bottom right were developed and all those in the top left underdeveloped. Similarly, those in the top right were pro-Western and those in the bottom left pro-Communist. Noting these facts Wish then concluded that the real axes or dimensions of his model were economic development and political alignment.[4] My aim here is to discover whether there are similarly fundamental and revealing axes or dimensions within Kierkegaard's authorship and, further, whether the aberrant frequency lists for our new groups of books will enable us to describe these dimensions with more certainty and precision.

It may be granted at the outset that there seems little hope of identifying such axes on the basis of any superficial account of the groups already mentioned. What, after all, is common between a group of early pseudonymous works and another group most of which seem primarily concerned with the attack on the church? Again, what is common between works devoted primarily to literary and cultural comment and criticism and those whose chief concern appears to be the edification of the reader? In an attempt to answer these questions we now turn to the aberrant frequency words for these groups, comparable samples of which are given in tables 6a-d.

Unfortunately there are a number of serious obstacles to this apparently simple undertaking. There are approximately 400 aberrant frequency words in each of these groups and it is plainly impossible either to reproduce these lists in their entirety or to provide the detailed analysis which they require and, indeed, deserve. Instead, I have had to be content with showing for each group the first 55 positive aberrant frequency words and, by way of contrast, 5 of the highest negative ones. This is only a small fraction of the available evidence but it is plainly out of the question to show all of it. In any event, I am sure that the reader who studies the accompanying lists carefully will see that our interpretations are not without supporting evidence.

The selection of aberrant frequency words for group 1 is shown in table 6a. As might be expected, this list reflects the distinctive characteristics, emphases and categories of the early pseudonymous authorship. It contains many terms associated with the aesthetic, the ethical and the religious stages as well as Sphære (sphere or stage), the latter with 95 occurrences and 6.81 standard deviations. However, a closer inspection of either the original or the printed version of this list suggests that the real focus of this group is the aesthetic as such. This is borne out by the large proportion of words denoting essentially aesthetic concepts and, equally, the significantly low frequencies of Gode, Christus, Gud and, for that matter, of vi and Menneske. In short, we conclude that this group represents the aesthetic stage and note in support of this conclusion Kierkegaard's own habit of referring to the whole of the early pseudonymous authorship as his aesthetic production.[5]

A comparable list of aberrant frequency words for group 2 is shown in table 6b. At first glance this group appears concerned mainly with the attack upon the church; note, for example, the emphasis upon the Christianity of the New Testament, the many references to Martensen and Mynster, and the frequent mention of the church and its priests. Again, however, closer inspection shows that this is but part of the story. Indeed, it reveals a clear and marked emphasis upon the conception of Christianity underlying that attack. This is evident from the significantly high frequency of one or more forms of all of the following: Christendom, Christus, Høiheden, drage, Sandhedsvidne, Forargelse, ædru, Fornedrelse, lide, Ubetingede, Samtidighedens, Forbilledet, Gudsdrykelse, Forkyndelse, Beundrer, Selfornægtelse, etc. I suggest, then, that the fundamental focus of this group is not the attack upon the church as such but rather the underlying conception of Christianity of which that attack is a natural expression. It is about that form of Christianity which is identified as religiousness B or, put another way, the fourth and last of the existence-stages.

The purpose of this excursion was to identify the first dimension of our model. We have already argued that the first group represents the aesthetic element in Kierkegaard's authorship and the second the explicitly or, better, the unconditionally Christian. I therefore conclude that this is best described as the "spheres" or "stages" dimension of the authorship and cite in support of this conclusion Kierkegaard's own later four-fold account of the stages and, particularly, the view expressed in AE that in the final analysis the real choice is between the aesthetic and the Christian with the aesthetic, the ethical and religiousness A included within but nevertheless made subservient to Christianity.[6]

Our earlier description of group 3 as primarily literary and cultural comment and criticism is clearly supported by both the list shown in table 6c and its original much longer version. Indeed, both show a high proportion of places, titles, and names, both real and fictional. But, equally obviously, both show many of the key concepts and categories of Kierkegaard's social thought, especially the more negative and critical ones. Note, for example, the various forms of the following: Publikum, Nutiden, Nivelleringen, Tidsalderens, Revolutions-Tiden, Reflexion, Mængde, Reflexion, Categorie, Existeren, lidenskabsløs, Reflex, Pressen, Politik, Livs-Anskuelse, Instantsen, Individerne, Sandsebedrag, Formløshed, Blad, extensivt,

Institutioner, Demoralisation, Numeriske, Politiske, nivelleres, etc. In fact, these lists also contain traces of the positive or constructive aspect of his social thought such as the following: Enkelte, religieus, opbyggelige, Menneske-Lighed, Religieusitetens, and ethisk-religieust. But for Kierkegaard the real solution to the urgent social problems of his time is to be found not in any merely secular thought and analysis but instead in the specifically religious. Without wishing to beg the question, we note that this is at least suggested by the fact that such key religious terms as Kjerlighed, Menneske, Gud and Du show a very significant deficiency in group 3 but a very significant excess for group 4 the short version of which is shown in table 6d.

It is obvious from the lists for this group that, as everyone knows, the works in question are edifying and devotional discourses; indeed, these lists contain many words reflecting the peculiarly direct and intimate nature of such discourses. But they also contain many of the key terms in Kierkegaard's constructive or religious solution to the problems of his time and, he did not doubt, of society in general. In fact, just as he assumed that the real problems of society were best presented within the context of literary criticism so too he assumed that they could only be solved within religion. For Kierkegaard, it was a sheer confusion to attempt to solve such problems "in the medium of worldliness . . . the nature of which is difference and inequality."[7] He also held that his age was profoundly mistaken in assuming that real improvement could be achieved through mere change of structures and organizations. His own quite different view is clearly stated in his third preface to the piece now known in English as On Authority and Revelation: "The problem is a religious, a Christian problem, and, as I have said, it has already been solved. For give us eternity, a prospect of eternity every instant, its seriousness and its blessedness, its relief; give eternity again to every individual—— then no more blood-shedding will be needed, . . ."[8] In fact, Kierkegaard sees the political simply as a modern abbreviation or foreshortening of the religious and the real problem of society as the lack of moral sanity among its members. This moral sanity, he believes, is possible only within traditional Christianity, which alone provides an adequate framework for a truly human existence, puts worldly matters in their proper perspective, and takes human equality seriously. This view is assumed throughout these works and is reflected in the significantly high frequency of the following words: Kjerlighed, Gud, Du, Fuglen, Gode, Menneske, elske, Lilien, Kjerlige, Næsten, Bekymring, Forventning, Evighed, Evige, Sjel, Lydighed, Taalmodighed, Gave, Alteret, Tvesindethed, Bekymrede, Trøst, Barmhjertighed, jordiske, ubetinget, Apostelen, Glædelige, Verden, Evangeliet, Timelighed, etc. I believe that those familiar with Kierkegaard's writings will recognize these words as representing important elements of that framework which, according to Kierkegaard, alone fosters and supports right relations with the neighbour. We can therefore see these works as providing Kierkegaard's solution to problems which we still perhaps regard as social but which he recognized as fundamentally religious.

Before proceeding to describe the dimension joining groups 3 and 4 I pause for a moment to deal with two matters related to our description of the last group.

It is widely assumed that Kierkegaard has no social thought, or that, at best, he is some kind of extreme and reactionary individualist. But it is no longer necessary to be taken in by such superficial impressions since the linguistic evidence clearly indicates the contrary. For example, the fact that vi shows +11.57 standard deviations while mig and jeg show -29.83 and -46.75 reflects the strong underlying sense of community which pervades these works. Note that, by contrast, these last two words are first and fourth in the aesthetic group with +39.01 and +24.05 standard deviations, respectively. It should hardly be necessary to remind the reader that Kierkegaard dismissed these works as a duplicity but it may be worth pointing out that he recognized communism as but another species of aesthetic individualism and rejected it as such.[9]

Our claim that group 4 gives Kierkegaard's solution to social problems invites the question whether his solution is specifically Christian or more broadly religious. The answer is not easy since there appears to be evidence on both sides. For example, there is Kierkegaard's own remark concerning the problems of his time: " . . . which only Christianity can solve and has solved long ago."[10] On the other hand, CT is the only work in this group which is specifically Christian in both title and content. Further, many of the words we have cited as representing aspects of this solution, though originally Christian, have now become part of the more general western religious tradition and often seem to be associated in Kierkegaard's mind with religiousness A. Again, Christus shows -3.69 standard deviations in this group and Christendom -12.75. It would seem therefore that while Kierkegaard may have conceived his solution as specifically Christian he is not anxious or jealous to represent it explicitly as such. Put another way, he is much less concerned that Christianity should receive credit in this regard than that man should recover that framework which alone makes true social existence possible.

But to return to the problem before us. We have already described groups 3 and 4 as presenting Kierkegaard's social thought with the former emphasizing its negative or critical and the latter its positive or constructive aspects. It seems therefore that the line joining these groups is most appropriately called the social thought axis or dimension of his thought.

We have identified and named two separate and distinct axes in Kierkegaard's works but it is of course possible that there might be others and that those we have identified might be described in other and perhaps yet more revealing ways. However, this is the best we have been able to do on the basis of the present evidence and we conclude therefore that the stages and social thought dimensions constitute the main axes in the framework of his authorship. Note that this account does not commit Kierkegaard to anything which might be described as a belief in the doctrine of the stages (whatever that might be) nor does it mean that Christianity is less central to his thought than many of us have always supposed. Note, too, that it is consistent with his emphasis upon what it means to exist, his conception of himself as a "thinker," and his preoccupation with the problems of his time and their real and lasting solution.

It is perhaps worth noting that the identification of these two as the fundamental dimensions of this authorship does not deny the existence or even the role and importance of works such as KK, G, TSA, and SD which appear to have but little relation to them. It does, however, suggest that these works, while important and interesting in themselves, are nevertheless peripheral to the main thrusts and intentions of Kierkegaard's authorship.

It is perhaps also worth noting that groups 2 and 4 are generally closer to the centre of our model than groups 1 and 3. This is consistent with Kierkegaard's claim that he was an essentially religious author and casts some doubt upon the intentions of those who, identifying Kierkegaard with his early pseudonymous works, scavenge his carcass for their own philosophical purposes. Note, too, that Ø is both very close to the centre of our model and more or less directly on one of its main dimensions. Plainly then we cannot dismiss the attack on the church as an aberration or this work as tangential to the authorship.

I conclude this part of our study by noting that it is now possible to locate within the space of our model not only Kierkegaard's actual works but also some which, for one reason or another, he never actually completed. Consider, for example, his unfinished reply to L. G. M. Gude's Om Mag. Kierkegaards Forfattervirksomed. Iagttagelser af en Landsbypræsten (On Dr. Kierkegaard's Authorship. Observations of a Country Parson) from the various drafts[11] of which we have been able to identify its aberrant frequency words. This long list clearly shows that this work combines an account of the authorship with the beginnings of an attack upon the priests. This is confirmed by a comparison of this list with the top 100 aberrant frequency words for all of the even remotely similar works in the corpus which shows that it shares 15 with FV, 14 with SFV, 11 with Ø, and 4 with B21. In short, had Kierkegaard been able to complete and publish this work it would have appeared in our model suspended between these four, more or less directly above B21, and midway between the axes we have already identified. That we can thus now locate this unfinished piece is part of what we mean when we refer to this study as giving us something of the shape and structure of Kierkegaard's authorship.

Of course I hope that this account will give all of us a better appreciation of the richness and complexity of Kierkegaard's authorship and that none of us will be tempted in the future simply to identify him with one or other part of his extremely varied production or, yet worse, with one or other of his particular works. However, this must be obvious and I close on another and quite different note.

I believe that the account I have given of the shape and structure of Kierkegaard's works is in some sense essentially correct; indeed, I would not have offered it if I did not think so. At the same time I am all too acutely aware that even the data of this study is itself genuinely 33-dimensional, that I have attempted to represent all this information in but three dimensions, and that my account cannot therefore be literally true and must at best be some kind of simplification. More positively, I suggest that we not ask whether this model is literally true but rather whether it will help us to grasp all these complex relations in their totality and serve as a basis from which we can now proceed to articulate other and more accurate ones. I have made a first move and now invite you to join the search.

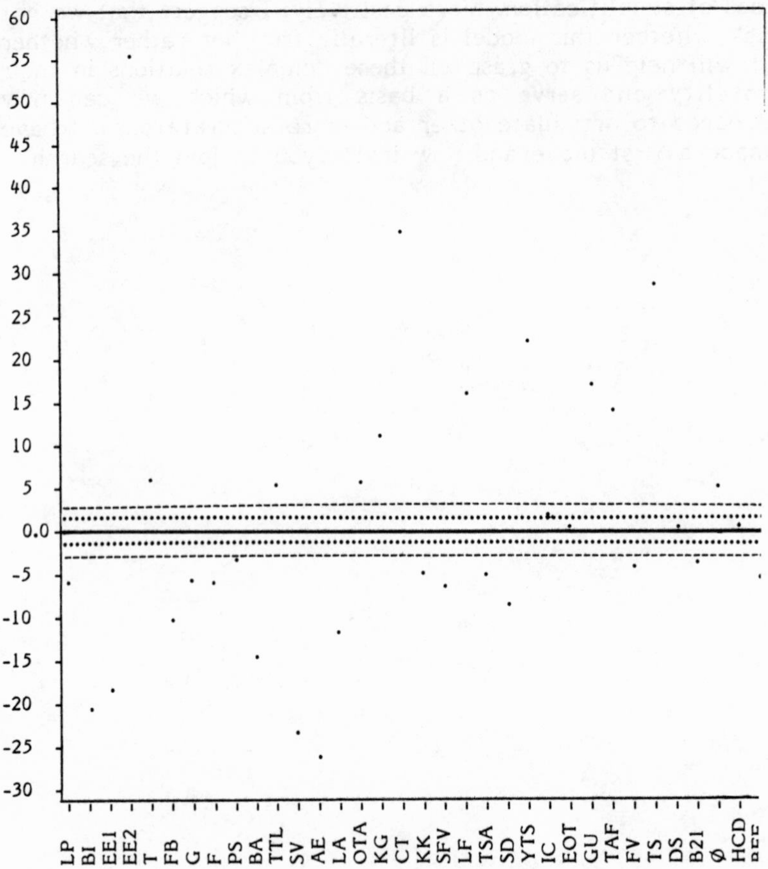

Figure 1. Standard deviations of Du in works of corpus

Table 1. Types, tokens, ABFREQ words, etc.
in each work of corpus

Title	A Types	B Tokens	C ABFREQ words	D C as % of A
LP	3974	16091	1482	37.29
BI	13266	105509	2751	20.74
EE1	14269	154518	2206	15.46
EE2	11167	132630	1338	11.98
FB	5754	40822	1234	21.45
G	5809	32343	1284	22.10
T	9946	128854	1845	18.55
F	4455	22088	1132	25.41
PS	4769	34799	1094	22.94
BA	6994	53048	1125	16.09
TTL	4762	32196	1030	21.63
SV	15996	173007	1777	11.11
AE	15481	214013	2058	13.29
LA	6638	36159	1752	26.39
OTA	9325	119820	1530	16.41
KG	10000	142455	1577	15.77
CT	7945	103179	1279	16.10
KK	1987	7906	683	34.37
SFV	4721	32465	990	20.97
LF	2154	15293	535	24.84
TSA	2873	17351	683	23.77
SD	5018	43603	1043	20.79
YTS	1614	9486	442	27.39
IC	7394	82674	1058	14.31
EOT	977	4019	280	28.66
GU	1167	4926	336	28.79
TAF	1358	6704	362	26.66
FV	1300	4567	438	33.69
TS	3848	26614	810	21.08
DS	5057	40957	1154	22.82
B21	3806	23430	1163	30.56
Ø	6929	58731	1333	19.24
HCD	895	3034	306	34.19
BFF	3981	18741	1123	28.21

Table 2a. Words showing => 20.00 standard deviations in FB

Word	Trans./Use	A.F.	R.F.	S.D.
Abraham	Abraham	231	56.6	97.26
Isaak	Isaac	111	27.2	69.21
Almene	universal	104	25.5	44.57
Agnete	Agnes	40	9.8	42.16
Sara	Sarah	35	8.6	38.81
Havmanden	merman (def.)	29	7.1	36.36
Abrahams	Abraham's	35	8.6	35.86
Ridder	knight	50	12.2	32.86
Helt	hero	70	17.1	30.56
Kniven	knife (def.)	18	4.4	26.43
Agamemnon	Agamemnon	14	3.4	25.26
Troens	faith, belief (gen.)	76	18.6	24.88
tragiske	tragic (adj.)	39	9.6	24.63
Iphigenia	Iphigenia	12	2.9	23.39
Troen	faith, belief (def.)	109	26.7	22.52
Morija	Moriah	10	2.4	21.35
Absurde	(the) absurd	31	7.6	21.30
han	he	1018	249.4	21.08
Enkelte	(that) individual	103	25.2	20.84
Morijabjerget	Mount Moriah	9	2.2	20.26

There are 1,234 ABFREQ word-types in FB

Table 2b. Words showing => 15.00 standard deviations in T

Word	Trans./Use	A.F.	R.F.	S.D.
Forventning	expectation	150	11.6	34.04
Taalmodigheden	patience	99	7.7	33.77
Gave	gift	156	12.1	31.74
Sjel	soul	200	15.5	28.64
Taalmodighed	patience	98	7.6	28.49
da	then, when, since	1367	106.1	24.21
Feigheden	cowardice	48	3.7	22.74
Synders	sinner's	59	4.6	22.63
han	he	2597	201.5	22.41
Ordet	word (def.)	138	10.7	21.88
ovenfra	from above	37	2.9	21.71
Job	Job	73	5.7	21.71
Herren	Master, Lord	83	6.4	20.79
ham	him	1111	86.2	20.60
Forventningen	expectation	47	3.6	20.56
Opfyldelsen	fulfillment	50	3.9	20.52
Ungdommen	youth (def.)	66	5.1	20.25
Vidnesbyrd	testimony	58	4.5	19.94
Gaven	gift, present	43	3.3	19.56
apostoliske	apostolic	44	3.4	18.93
fuldkommen	perfect	98	7.6	18.72
forventer	expect	33	2.6	18.63
Sjelen	soul (def.)	66	5.1	18.52
var	was	1199	93.1	18.11
Anna	Anna	33	2.6	18.10
Himlens	heaven (gen.)	52	4.0	17.28
Gud	God	640	49.7	17.18
erhverve	acquire	60	4.7	17.14
indvortes	inner, inward	58	4.5	17.08
Mangfoldighed	multitude	89	6.9	16.03
Bedende	praying one	32	2.5	15.94
Menneske	man	659	51.1	15.94
eies	be owned	20	1.6	15.35
Forventningens	expectation's	24	1.9	15.30
Bønnen	prayer (def.)	39	3.0	15.12
Erhvervelsen	acquisition	21	1.6	15.02
Prædikeren	the Preacher	24	1.9	15.01

There are 1,845 ABFREQ word-types in T

Table 2c. Words showing => 15.00 standard deviations in OTA

Word	Trans./Use	A.F.	R.F.	S.D.
Gode	(the) Good	430	35.9	44.91
Lidende	the suffering	185	15.4	35.29
Tvesindethed	double-mindedness	78	6.5	32.89
Eet	one	231	19.3	32.37
Trængselen	crowd, throng	104	8.7	28.77
Tvesindede	double-minded	41	3.4	24.19
Byrde	burden	74	6.2	24.11
Bekymrede	the sorrowful	63	5.3	23.45
Tvesindetheden	double-mindedness	36	3.0	22.67
Næringssorg	financial worry	38	3.2	22.62
Lidelsen	suffering	102	8.5	22.16
Veien	way, road (def.)	150	12.5	22.02
tvesindet	is double-minded	36	3.0	21.98
Lilierne	lilies (def.)	47	3.9	21.87
Vei	way, road	175	14.6	20.22
Byrden	burden (def.)	39	3.3	20.21
Lidelser	sufferings	77	6.4	18.41
Klogskaben	cleverness	42	3.5	18.29
forskaffer	provide, procure	25	2.1	17.71
Afgjørelsen	decision	62	5.2	17.50
ville	will	352	29.4	17.47
Himmelens	heaven's	33	2.8	17.24
Glædelige	the joyful	41	3.4	17.20
Frimodigheden	frankness	25	2.1	16.69
tunge	heavy (adj., pl.)	38	3.2	16.50
Evigheden	eternity (def.)	141	11.8	16.45
Straffen	punishment	48	4.0	16.31
Lønnen	reward (def.)	35	2.9	16.10
skyldig	guilty	76	6.3	15.80
veie	weigh (inf.)	19	1.6	15.55

There are 1,530 ABFREQ word-types in OTA

Table 2d. Words showing => 25.50 standard deviations in HCD

Word	Trans./Use	A.F.	R.F.	S.D.
Grave	sepulchres	14	46.1	81.09
Propheternes	prophets'	10	33.0	67.47
Gravsteder	tombs	7	23.1	66.83
Fædres	fathers' (gen.)	9	29.7	63.01
Blod-Skyld	blood-guilt	7	23.1	62.50
Propheterne	prophets	7	23.1	50.99
pryde	garnish (inf.)	6	19.8	50.48
Retfærdiges	the righteous'	7	23.1	48.98
ihjelsloge (s.v.)	be killed	3	9.9	43.75
sloge (s.v.)	beat, kill	8	26.4	42.97
bygge	build (inf.)	13	42.8	40.80
deelagtige	involved	3	9.9	37.87
Beroligende	reassuring	3	9.9	33.86
Modparten	opposition	4	13.2	33.61
rødme	blush (inf.)	5	16.5	31.47
Hykleriets	hypocrisy's	3	9.9	30.89
Idealer	ideals	3	9.9	30.89
samtykke	consent, agree	4	13.2	29.08
Hyklerie	hypocrisy	6	19.8	27.98
Christendom	Christianity	3	98.9	25.89

There are 306 ABFREQ word-types in HCD

	LP	BI	EE1	EE2	FB	G	T	F	PS	BA	TTL	SV	AE	LA	OTA	KG	CT	KK	SFV	LF	TSA	SD	YTS	IC	EOT	GU	TAF	FV	TS	DS	B21	Ø	HCD
BI	176																																
EE1	104	360																															
EE2	76	300	383																														
FB	31	92	110	103																													
G	47	82	160	102	81																												
T	34	158	186	197	121	77																											
F	48	71	77	64	40	61	60																										
PS	41	109	55	55	61	35	99	44																									
BA	74	230	157	139	80	70	108	65	95																								
TTL	26	59	59	75	55	38	184	37	62	62																							
SV	48	176	302	210	104	146	184	62	71	115	97																						
AE	45	266	198	174	82	45	136	76	118	210	78	243																					
LA	60	114	114	67	54	54	45	57	49	94	59	99	146																				
OTA	15	113	107	130	55	29	380	26	60	74	142	114	136	56																			
KG	28	120	129	138	43	21	279	26	57	84	124	114	156	64	320																		
CT	17	94	84	99	28	23	271	27	46	61	102	87	111	29	327	276																	
KK	25	30	49	30	14	22	16	20	16	33	18	41	41	46	23	28	29																
SFV	49	70	48	42	36	43	42	54	40	48	44	73	102	66	47	74	64	38															
LF	18	37	37	30	19	11	71	11	22	32	48	21	34	19	91	69	84	10	28														
TSA	23	48	25	23	29	16	26	24	36	37	20	21	81	28	36	51	45	26	52	18													
SD	34	101	52	49	33	21	47	16	58	112	46	50	115	55	59	93	78	29	58	34	45												
YTS	13	21	31	27	22	25	71	12	20	17	37	30	15	15	56	47	67	14	26	32	20	31											
IC	28	109	79	74	40	23	143	21	70	53	56	69	140	43	170	170	215	26	86	54	71	98	63										
EOT	6	14	15	14	13	11	39	8	11	9	20	18	10	11	25	26	39	9	21	21	14	21	42	28									
GU	8	9	14	15	11	7	72	6	15	6	31	12	12	13	53	34	40	7	8	23	13	11	21	21	12								
TAF	8	16	15	19	13	8	50	8	13	11	31	12	9	3	41	46	56	8	12	23	21	21	49	36	29	22							
FV	22	24	26	20	8	15	13	28	10	24	12	20	51	25	11	13	17	14	94	12	23	19	14	38	9	3	10						
TS	19	32	47	47	26	34	67	27	24	22	44	49	32	28	70	69	85	12	54	38	36	37	36	90	27	22	31	18					
DS	30	68	50	53	26	26	74	33	41	35	48	46	77	39	119	109	111	17	82	65	43	71	41	158	25	21	19	35	126				
B21	38	51	41	33	22	26	41	44	20	25	28	48	63	32	36	50	46	29	79	30	30	39	18	77	16	11	18	40	54	96			
Ø	54	119	98	92	30	34	98	35	47	78	58	88	140	55	108	141	143	31	98	50	60	96	38	172	20	26	29	39	95	211	203		
HCD	9	10	12	11	4	8	16	10	3	6	4	11	13	4	11	15	14	4	16	9	19	7	11	26	10	6	15	13	25	29	52	71	
BFF	48	51	77	45	19	35	19	68	24	26	22	61	69	58	14	25	14	40	50	15	29	17	8	32	6	8	8	24	31	32	69	47	12

Table 3a. Number of ABFREQ words common to each pair of books

	LP	BI	EE1	EE2	FB	G	T	F	PS	BA	TTL	SV	AE	LA	OTA	KG	CT
BI	4.34																
EE1	2.90	7.83															
EE2	2.77	7.92	12.12														
FB	1.15	2.36	3.30	4.17													
G	1.73	2.07	4.80	4.05	3.32												
T	1.03	3.56	4.81	6.60	4.09	2.52											
F	1.87	1.86	2.36	2.66	1.72	2.59	2.06										
PS	1.62	2.92	1.69	2.31	2.69	1.49	3.49	2.02									
BA	2.92	6.31	4.95	5.98	3.51	2.99	3.77	2.97	4.47								
TTL	1.05	1.59	1.86	3.27	2.49	1.67	6.84	1.74	3.01	2.96							
SV	1.49	4.04	8.20	7.23	3.58	5.01	5.35	2.18	2.54	4.13	3.58						
AE	1.29	5.86	4.87	5.40	2.55	1.36	3.61	2.44	3.89	7.06	2.59	6.77					
LA	1.89	2.60	2.97	2.22	1.84	1.81	1.27	2.02	1.75	3.38	2.17	2.89	3.98				
OTA	0.50	2.71	2.95	4.75	2.03	1.04	12.69	0.99	2.34	2.87	5.87	3.57	3.94	1.74			
KG	0.92	2.85	3.53	4.97	1.55	0.74	8.88	0.97	2.18	3.21	4.99	3.52	4.48	1.96	11.48		
CT	0.62	2.39	2.47	3.93	1.13	0.91	9.50	1.13	1.98	2.60	4.62	2.93	3.44	0.97	13.17	10.70	
KK	1.17	0.88	1.73	1.51	0.74	1.13	0.64	1.11	0.91	1.86	1.06	1.69	1.52	1.93	1.05	1.25	1.50
SFV	2.02	1.91	1.52	1.84	1.65	1.93	1.50	2.61	1.96	2.32	2.23	2.71	3.46	2.47	1.90	2.97	2.90
LF	0.90	1.14	1.37	1.63	1.09	0.61	3.07	0.66	1.37	1.97	3.16	0.92	1.33	0.84	4.61	3.38	4.86
TSA	1.07	1.42	0.87	1.15	1.54	0.82	1.04	1.34	2.07	2.09	1.18	0.86	3.05	1.16	1.65	2.31	2.35
SD	1.36	2.73	1.63	2.10	1.47	0.91	1.65	0.74	2.79	5.45	2.27	1.81	3.85	2.01	2.35	3.68	3.48
YTS	0.68	0.66	1.18	1.54	1.33	1.47	3.20	0.77	1.32	1.10	2.58	1.37	0.60	0.69	2.92	2.38	4.05
IC	1.11	2.95	2.48	3.19	1.78	0.99	5.18	0.97	3.36	2.49	2.76	2.49	4.70	1.55	7.03	6.90	10.13
EOT	0.34	0.46	0.61	0.87	0.87	0.71	1.87	0.57	0.81	0.64	1.55	0.88	0.43	0.54	1.40	1.42	2.57
GU	0.44	0.29	0.55	0.90	0.71	0.43	3.41	0.41	1.06	0.41	2.32	0.57	0.50	0.63	2.92	1.81	2.54
TAF	0.44	0.52	0.59	1.13	0.82	0.49	2.32	0.54	0.90	0.75	2.28	0.56	0.37	0.14	2.22	2.43	3.53
FV	1.16	0.76	0.99	1.14	0.48	0.88	0.57	1.82	0.66	1.56	0.82	0.91	2.09	1.15	0.56	0.65	1.00
TS	0.84	0.91	1.58	2.24	1.29	1.65	2.59	1.41	1.28	1.15	2.45	1.93	1.13	1.10	3.08	2.98	4.24
DS	1.15	1.77	1.51	2.17	1.10	1.08	2.53	1.46	1.86	1.56	2.25	1.59	2.46	1.36	4.64	4.16	4.78
B21	1.46	1.32	1.23	1.34	0.93	1.07	1.38	1.95	0.89	1.10	1.29	1.66	1.99	1.11	1.35	1.86	1.92
Ø	1.96	3.00	2.85	3.57	1.18	1.32	3.18	1.44	1.97	3.28	2.52	2.91	4.31	1.82	3.92	5.09	5.79
HCD	0.51	0.33	0.48	0.67	0.26	0.51	0.75	0.70	0.21	0.42	0.30	0.53	0.55	0.19	0.60	0.80	0.89
BFF	1.88	1.33	2.37	1.86	0.81	1.48	0.64	3.11	1.09	1.17	1.03	2.15	2.22	2.06	0.53	0.93	0.59

	KK	SFV	LF	TSA	SD	YTS	IC	EOT	GU	TAF	FV	TS	DS	B21	Ø	HCD
SFV	2.32															
LF	0.83	1.87														
TSA	1.94	3.21	1.50													
SD	1.71	2.94	2.20	2.68												
YTS	1.26	1.85	3.39	1.81	2.13											
IC	1.52	4.38	3.51	4.25	4.89	4.38										
EOT	0.94	1.68	2.64	1.48	1.61	6.18	2.14									
GU	0.69	0.61	2.71	1.29	0.80	2.77	1.53	1.99								
TAF	0.77	0.90	2.63	2.05	1.52	6.49	2.60	4.73	3.25							
FV	1.26	7.05	1.25	2.09	1.30	1.62	2.61	1.27	0.39	1.27						
TS	0.81	3.09	2.91	2.47	2.04	2.96	5.06	2.54	1.96	2.72	1.46					
DS	0.93	3.98	4.00	2.40	3.34	2.64	7.69	1.77	1.43	1.27	2.25	6.86				
B21	1.60	3.81	1.80	1.65	1.80	1.13	3.59	1.12	0.74	1.19	2.56	2.81	4.32			
Ø	1.56	4.40	2.75	3.07	4.21	2.19	7.75	1.26	1.58	1.74	2.25	4.64	9.27	8.85		
HCD	0.41	1.25	1.08	1.96	0.52	1.49	1.94	1.74	0.94	2.30	1.78	2.29	2.03	3.67	4.53	
BFF	2.27	2.42	0.91	1.63	0.79	0.51	1.49	0.43	0.55	0.54	1.56	1.63	1.43	3.11	1.95	0.85

Table 3b. Percentage of ABFREQ words common to each pair of books

Table 3c. Books showing most and least similarity to each other book in corpus

Title	Closest 1st	Closest 2nd	Furthest 32nd	Furthest 33rd
LP	BI	EE1	TAF[1]	EOT
BI	EE2	EE1	HCD	GU
EE1	EE2	SV	GU	HCD
EE2	EE1	BI	EOT	HCD
FB	EE2	T	FV	HCD
G	SV	EE1	TAF	GU
T	OTA	EE2	KK[2]	FV
F	BFF	EE2	EOT	GU
PS	BA	AE	FV	HCD
BA	AE	BI	HCD	GU
TTL	T	OTA	FV	HCD
SV	EE1	EE2	TAF	HCD
AE	BA	SV	EOT	TAF
LA	AE	BA	HCD	TAF
OTA	CT	KG	BFF	LP
KG	OTA	CT	HCD	FV
CT	OTA	KG	LP	BFF
KK	SFV	BFF	GU	HCD
SFV	FV	Ø	TAF	GU
LF	CT	OTA	F	G
TSA	IC	Ø	SV	G
SD	BA	IC	F	HCD
YTS	TAF	EOT	AE[3]	BFF
IC	CT	DS	G	F
EOT	YTS	TAF	AE	LP
GU	T	TAF	FV	BI
TAF	YTS	EOT	AE	LA
FV	SFV	IC	FB	GU
TS	DS	IC	LP	KK
DS	Ø	IC	G	KK
B21	Ø	DS	PS	GU
Ø	DS	B21	EOT	FB
HCD	Ø	B21	PS	LA
BFF	B21	F[4]	YTS	EOT

Notes to Table

1. Both TAF and GU show a similarity index of 0.44 with LP but the true values of these pairs are 0.4357298 and 0.4419889, respectively.
2. Both KK and BFF show a similarity index of 0.64 with T but the true values of these pairs are 0.6369426 and 0.6442861, respectively.
3. Both AE and BFF show a similarity index of 0.43 with EOT but the true values of these pairs are 0.429555 and 0.430725, respectively.
4. Both F and B21 show a similarity index of 3.11 with BFF but the true values of these pairs are 3.1123139 and 3.1092821, respectively.

Table 4. Coordinates and radii of three dimensional model

Title	x	y	z	radius
LP	-1.271	0.419	-0.129	13.44
BI	-0.862	-0.403	0.112	9.58
EE1	-0.744	-0.258	-0.285	8.37
EE2	-0.445	-0.333	-0.230	6.02
FB	-0.545	-0.916	-0.480	11.69
G	-0.742	-0.245	-0.984	12.57
T	0.120	-0.608	-0.272	6.77
F	0.759	0.417	-0.764	11.55
PS	-0.403	-0.804	0.512	10.35
BA	-0.627	-0.313	0.247	7.43
TTL	0.198	-0.741	-0.116	7.76
SV	-0.576	-0.376	-0.351	7.72
AE	-0.581	-0.128	0.350	6.90
LA	-1.047	0.032	0.542	11.79
OTA	0.307	-0.634	0.152	7.21
KG	0.193	-0.429	0.298	5.57
CT	0.434	-0.343	0.136	5.70
KK	-0.481	0.777	0.933	13.06
SFV	-0.164	0.589	0.137	6.27
LF	0.831	-0.259	0.428	9.70
TSA	0.361	0.508	0.746	9.72
SD	0.018	-0.137	0.841	8.52
YTS	0.952	-0.194	-0.300	10.17
IC	0.269	0.027	0.201	3.37
EOT	1.287	0.097	-0.438	13.63
GU	1.292	-0.781	0.004	15.10
TAF	1.342	-0.052	0.028	13.43
FV	0.118	1.256	0.124	12.68
TS	0.540	0.191	-0.465	7.38
DS	0.405	0.312	0.047	5.13
B21	0.146	0.882	-0.342	9.57
Ø	0.134	0.263	0.011	2.95
HCD	1.080	1.153	-0.442	16.40
BFF	-0.780	1.027	-0.251	13.14

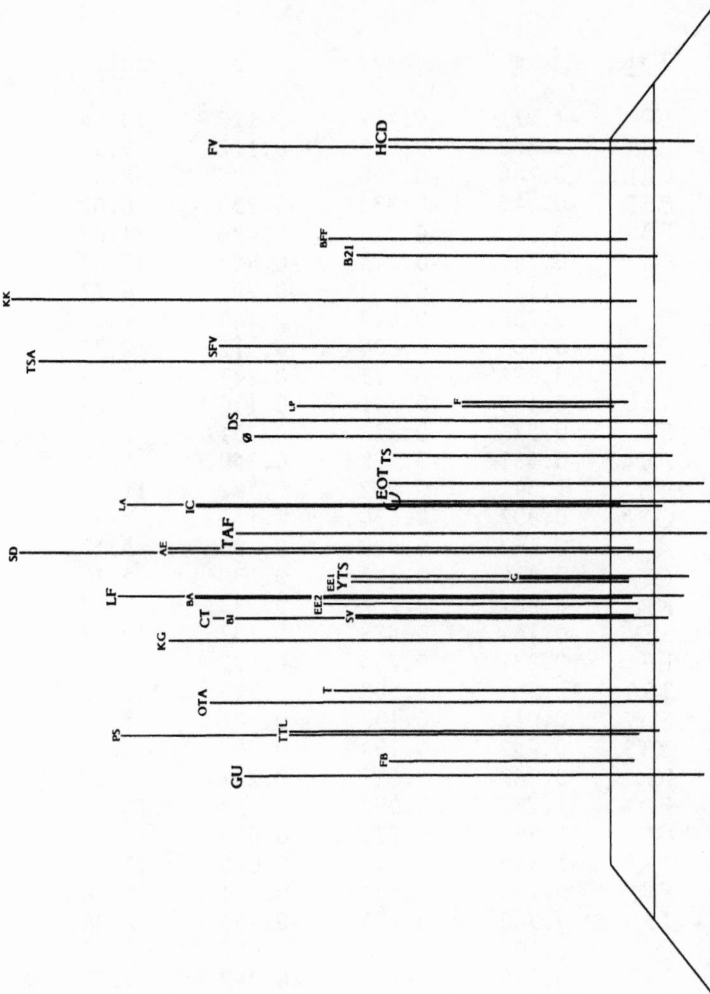

Figure 2. Model of Kierkegaard's Authorship (ABFREQ words |S.D.|=> 2.58)

Table 5a. Top 40 ABFREQ words common to EE1 and EE2

Word	Trans./Use	EE1 A.F.	EE1 S.D.	EE2 A.F.	EE2 S.D.
jeg	I (l.c.)	2415	33.2	1761	21.2
Kjærlighed	love	178	11.9	397	41.4
mig	me, myself	1161	28.0	653	9.7
Sjæl	soul	114	13.3	136	19.2
hende	her	764	40.6	247	6.1
Jeg	I (cap.)	362	19.6	246	12.2
har	has, have	1492	11.6	1413	15.1
bestandig	constantly	145	14.0	108	10.4
Gud	God	43	-17.7	196	-7.7
egentlig	real, proper	112	11.4	104	11.9
min	my, mine	495	17.0	298	6.8
Kjerlighed	love	0	-11.1	0	-10.3
han	he	1266	-16.7	1442	-6.9
Skjønhed	beauty	45	6.8	70	14.6
Pige	girl	270	28.7	72	3.5
første	first	168	6.8	218	14.2
Angst	dread	48	10.9	37	8.8
imidlertid	meanwhile	114	12.9	71	7.1
altid	always	237	8.7	224	10.0
Men	But	159	-11.0	181	-7.7
Socrates	Socrates	0	-9.5	0	-8.8
Thi	For	3	-9.5	5	-8.5
Betydning	meaning, sense	129	7.2	139	10.3
hvad	what	397	-9.8	383	-7.3
just	just, exactly	8	-8.9	10	-7.9
Christen	Christian	0	-8.8	2	-8.0
Christendommen	Christianity	19	-8.7	17	-8.0
Sorgen	sorrow (def.)	66	13.9	29	4.9
ung	young	141	21.7	37	2.8
jo	yes, certainly	245	-10.4	288	-5.8
ligger	lie, sleep	173	6.4	179	9.1
Christendom	Christianity	0	-7.9	1	-7.2
Individ	individual	65	7.4	59	7.5
forstaae	understand	30	-7.4	20	-7.5
Sandselige	sensuous	27	8.8	19	6.3
æsthetisk	aesthetic	55	3.4	116	15.8
Moment	moment	60	7.0	56	7.5
ahne	suspect	21	9.5	12	5.3
indre	interior	40	9.2	25	5.4
deri	in it, therein	96	5.2	113	9.2

There are 383 common ABFREQ words in EE1 and EE2

Table 5b. Top 40 ABFREQ words common to FB and T

		FB		T	
Word	Trans./Use	A.F.	S.D.	A.F.	S.D.
han	he	1018	21.1	2597	22.4
da	then, when	390	10.8	1367	24.2
Sjæl	soul	46	12.0	80	9.3
havde	had	152	8.3	457	13.4
ham	him	265	5.3	1111	20.6
saa	saw; so; sow	216	-8.2	744	-12.7
er	is, are	967	-5.9	2745	-15.5
sin	his, her(s)	216	7.4	655	11.8
var	was, were	296	4.6	1199	18.1
hans	his	144	4.5	567	14.4
Nøden	distress	11	12.2	10	5.2
Fader	father	28	7.5	62	7.8
Herren	the Lord	9	2.7	83	20.8
mig	me, myself	98	-3.4	101	-16.0
skulde	should	94	4.4	350	11.7
Christendommen	Christianity	2	-5.1	0	-9.6
thi	for	217	7.1	550	6.0
der	who, which	639	4.1	2138	10.2
Udfaldet	result, issue	19	12.4	14	3.2
prøvede	proved, tested	4	6.1	8	6.5
Ønske	wish, desire	17	3.7	73	10.6
Store	Great	21	9.8	23	3.9
end	than; to	187	3.7	662	10.0
just	just, exactly	1	-4.8	10	-7.8
Christen	Christian	0	-4.5	1	-8.0
Stund	while; hour	7	4.4	23	8.2
aarle	early	6	6.9	9	5.1
stred	fought	6	7.7	7	4.3
forstaaeligt	understandingly	4	6.6	6	5.0
Nød	distress	6	2.7	38	12.2
Kraft	strength	55	10.9	64	2.9
ikke	not	764	2.8	2699	11.1
Hvis	If, In case	22	5.4	51	5.8
modtog	received	5	4.0	17	7.7
Christendom	Christianity	0	-4.1	1	-7.1
Paulun	tent	2	5.8	3	4.6
Socrates	Socrates	9	-3.0	0	-8.7
som	who, whom; as	338	-5.4	1245	-4.8
forstaae	understand	58	5.6	132	4.6
blev	was	72	2.6	291	9.6

There are 121 common ABFREQ words in FB and T

Table 5c. Top 40 ABFREQ words common to T and OTA

Word	Trans./Use	T A.F.	T S.D.	OTA A.F.	OTA S.D.
jeg	I (l.c.)	271	-23.8	208	-24.4
Gode	(the) Good	143	8.6	430	44.9
han	he	2597	22.4	2123	14.2
da	then, when	1367	24.2	974	11.8
mig	me, myself	101	-16.0	76	-16.3
Gud	God	640	17.2	498	11.0
Menneske	man	659	15.9	516	10.1
den	it, he, she	3324	10.9	3194	12.6
hun	she	80	-11.7	69	-11.7
Ønsket	wish, desire	38	9.5	46	12.8
hende	her	39	-9.7	11	-11.4
Bekymrede	troubled (subs.)	18	4.6	63	23.5
Jeg	I (cap.)	5	-10.1	4	-9.8
min	my, mine	83	-8.1	33	-11.0
Bekymringen	concern (def.)	36	9.3	35	9.5
Talen	discourse (def.)	71	6.5	105	13.2
Herlighed	glory, splendour	46	7.8	55	10.8
har	has, have	517	-13.3	689	-5.7
gavnligt	profitable	23	7.3	29	10.4
af	of, by, from	718	-10.5	762	-7.2
dersom	if, in case	135	7.4	149	10.0
Socrates	Socrates	0	-8.7	0	-8.4
jo	yes, certainly	557	8.3	524	8.3
en	a, an, one	1696	-8.0	1551	-8.4
Christendommen	Christianity	0	-9.6	22	-6.9
Den	It, He, She	511	11.5	379	5.4
Fuldkommenhed	perfection	34	7.6	34	8.1
man	one, people	533	-9.3	565	-6.4
ham	him	1111	20.6	628	2.8
Overveielsen	reflection	21	9.4	14	6.0
ikke	not	2699	11.1	2255	5.1
apostoliske	apostolic	44	18.9	10	2.9
Sind	mind, disposition	52	8.9	39	6.2
Paulus	Paul	47	14.8	16	3.6
Mennesket	man (def.)	91	5.7	108	8.9
Verden	world	269	7.2	250	7.0
Faren	danger (def.)	50	12.4	22	4.0
Det	it, he, she	161	-8.9	201	-5.6
stakket	short-lived	8	4.5	16	10.9
Utaalmodigheden	impatience	23	14.1	7	3.5

There are 380 common ABFREQ words in T and OTA

Table 5d. Top 40 ABFREQ words common to PS and AE

Word	Trans./Use	PS A.F.	PS S.D.	AE A.F.	AE S.D.
Paradoxet	paradox (def.)	70	30.7	119	17.3
Guden	the God (def.)	158	73.0	57	5.7
historisk	historical	44	21.3	67	9.6
Væren	being	30	15.1	68	11.0
Generation	generation	31	20.5	37	7.0
hun	she	7	-7.8	68	-18.2
Historiske	historical (subs.)	40	27.6	27	4.5
Lærende	Learner	66	41.0	26	2.9
Dig	you, yourself	30	-5.7	45	-20.3
Du	you, thou	105	-4.1	139	-26.5
Socratiske	the Socratic	19	19.6	18	5.5
Paradox	paradox	15	8.3	64	13.0
Troen	faith (def.)	66	13.7	154	7.0
Sandheden	truth (def.)	51	9.9	172	9.2
Lidenskab	passion	29	5.0	212	16.4
hende	her	8	-5.4	26	-14.9
Uvished	uncertainty	10	7.5	37	10.0
absolut	absolute	28	5.5	169	13.2
Vanskeligheden	difficulty	14	5.7	78	12.3
Cap.	Chapter	7	5.9	35	11.5
Historisk	historical	5	4.5	39	14.9
Kjerlighed	love	0	-5.3	8	-12.5
relative	relative	6	4.4	46	14.2
Forstanden	reason (def.)	47	20.8	41	2.9
socratisk	Socratic (adj.)	21	19.6	14	3.0
cfr.	cf.	11	7.0	38	8.4
Modsigelse	contradiction	21	6.3	91	9.3
relativt	relatively	5	4.0	41	14.0
Troende	believer	21	8.2	57	6.2
evige	eternal	16	2.9	173	17.7
paradoxe	paradoxical	6	6.7	19	7.5
antage	assume (inf.)	23	7.6	71	6.6
Troens	faith (gen.)	22	6.1	90	8.0
Usandheden	lie, untruth	23	18.5	16	2.6
Vished	certainty	13	5.4	60	8.9
videre	further	25	3.8	179	12.4
Paradoxets	paradox (def., gen.)	5	9.1	8	4.9
Din	your, yours	5	-4.0	17	-11.0
Verden	world	13	-4.9	140	-8.7
eo	by that	10	5.1	45	8.2

There are 118 common ABFREQ words in PS and AE

Table 5e. List of ABFREQ words common to GU and HCD

		GU		HCD	
Word	Trans./Use	A.F.	S.D.	A.F.	S.D.
forandrende	changing	2	22.8	1	14.5
tryg	secure	2	4.7	4	12.6
vi	we	37	9.8	18	5.6
gode	good	8	7.4	4	4.5
Tænk	Consider	3	5.0	2	4.3
nei	no	6	3.0	6	4.5

There are 6 common ABFREQ words in GU and HCD

Table 6a. ABFREQ words in group 1 (EE1, EE2, BA, PS, SV, and AE.

Word	Trans./Use	Freq.	R.F.	S.D.
jeg	I (l.c.)	9196	120.68	39.01
hun	she	2959	38.83	33.18
hende	her, she	1923	25.24	30.83
mig	me, myself	3792	49.76	24.05
hendes	her, hers	889	11.67	20.44
min	my, mine	1774	23.28	18.11
en	a, an, one	14173	185.99	17.97
Don	Don	411	5.39	17.16
Jeg	I (cap.)	1090	14.30	16.58
Juan	Juan	369	4.84	16.26
Existerende	existing one	274	3.60	16.06
existerende	existing	276	3.62	16.05
Ægteskabet	marriage (def.)	303	3.98	15.60
Kjærlighed	love	668	8.77	15.46
Hun	She	446	5.85	15.03
Ethiske	(the) Ethical	337	4.42	15.02
existere	exist (inf.)	268	3.52	14.77
Individet	individual (def.)	399	5.24	14.74
ethisk	ethical	317	4.16	14.47
comisk	comic, comical	319	4.19	14.37
Existents	existence	362	4.75	14.36
absolute	absolute	358	4.70	14.06
Comiske	(the) comic	264	3.46	13.72
har	has, have	6461	84.79	13.67
Pige	girl	502	6.59	13.65
Religieuse	religious (subs.)	332	4.36	13.63
Guden	the God (def.)	230	3.02	13.52
Lidenskab	passion	471	6.18	13.31
Cordelia	Cordelia	165	2.17	12.46
Individ	individual	272	3.57	12.21
absolut	absolute	408	5.35	12.03
Charles	Charles	164	2.15	11.83
æsthetisk	aesthetic	319	4.19	11.31
Pathos	pathos	164	2.15	11.03
gjelder	concerns	264	3.46	10.86
Rinville	Rinville	119	1.56	10.58
Ægtemand	husband	154	2.02	10.53
Qvinden	woman (def.)	190	2.49	10.50
ethiske	ethical	163	2.14	10.24
Æsthetiske	aesthetic	163	2.14	10.24
eengang	once	278	3.65	10.24
mit	my, mine	670	8.79	10.23
man	one, you	5397	70.83	10.05
Paradoxet	paradox (def.)	199	2.61	10.01
Individualitet	individuality	152	1.99	9.83
Tænken	thought (def.)	121	1.59	9.80
bestandig	constantly	386	5.07	9.71
Subjektiviteten	subjectivity	104	1.36	9.57
religieuse	religious	207	2.72	9.54
et	a, an, one	6351	83.34	9.54
Musikken	music (def.)	101	1.33	9.53
Speculationen	speculation (def.)	112	1.47	9.46
Emmeline	Emmeline	93	1.22	9.35
Existentsen	existence (def.)	115	1.51	9.32
objektive	objective	101	1.33	9.21
Gode	the Good	175	2.30	-11.90
vi	we	862	11.31	-12.46
Christus	Christ	53	0.70	-14.28
Menneske	man	1456	19.11	-14.32
Gud	God	919	12.06	-23.23

Table 6b. ABFREQ words in group 2 (IC, Ø, DS, B21, and HCD)

Word	Trans./Use	Freq.	R.F.	S.D.
Christendom	Christianity	602	28.83	56.10
Christus	Christ	411	19.68	36.21
nye	new	319	15.28	35.87
Biskop	Bishop	173	8.28	35.05
Testamente	Testament	170	8.14	31.71
Testamentes	Testament's	133	6.37	31.24
Christen	Christian (subs.)	408	19.54	29.38
Christendommen	Christianity (def.)	507	24.28	29.07
Christenhed	Christendom	128	6.13	27.04
Christne	the Christians	284	13.60	27.00
Høiheden	loftiness	117	5.60	26.27
drage	draw (inf.)	137	6.56	24.90
Alle	all	347	16.62	24.58
Martensen	Martensen	80	3.83	24.34
Sandhedsvidne	witness...truth	80	3.83	24.34
christeligt	Christian (adj.)	150	7.18	24.02
Forargelsens	offence (gen.)	117	5.60	23.56
Mynster	Mynster	76	3.64	23.16
ædru	sober	91	4.36	23.02
Bestaaende	Establishment	109	5.22	22.72
Gud-Mennesket	(the) God-Man	81	3.88	21.85
Sandhedsvidner	witnesses...truth	63	3.02	21.60
Fornedrelse	abasement	65	3.11	20.58
lide	suffer (inf.)	173	8.28	20.15
forarges	be offended	91	4.36	19.87
Præsterne	priests	69	3.30	19.65
officielle	official	55	2.63	19.53
Christi	Christ (gen.)	129	6.18	19.46
bestaaende	established	57	2.73	18.73
hid	hither	75	3.59	18.48
Ubetingede	unconditional	60	2.87	18.45
Religion	religion	65	3.11	18.19
Præsten	priest (def.)	139	6.66	18.06
Fornedrede	offended	44	2.11	18.05
at	that; to	9188	439.98	17.71
Kirke	church	94	4.50	17.41
Præster	priests	67	3.21	17.39
just	just, exactly	325	15.56	17.28
Samtidighedens	contemporaneity	40	1.92	16.70
Eed	one	52	2.49	16.53
kongelig	royal	47	2.25	16.51
Læren	doctrine	77	3.69	16.49
Forbilledet	Model, Pattern	66	3.16	16.17
Jesus	Jesus	67	3.21	15.94
Fornedrelsen	abasement (def.)	34	1.63	15.87
Gudsdyrkelse	divine worship	50	2.39	15.79
Christenheden	Christendom (def.)	98	4.69	15.40
Forkyndelse	proclamation	49	2.35	15.27
Carriere	career	32	1.53	14.82
Levebrød	job, livelihood	54	2.59	14.60
Christendoms	Christianity's	31	1.48	14.57
Beundrer	admirers	34	1.63	14.32
Millioner	millions	59	2.83	14.20
Selvfornægtelse	self-denial	40	1.92	14.19
Pige	girl	13	0.62	-7.19
Hun	She	2	0.14	-7.55
hendes	her, hers	9	0.43	-10.34
hende	her	20	0.96	-15.03
hun	she	63	3.02	-18.10

Table 6c. ABFREQ words in group 3 (LP, LA, BFF, SFV, and FV)

Word	Trans./Use	Freq.	R.F.	S.D.
Andersen	Andersen	98	9.07	39.42
Forfatter	author	160	14.81	32.08
Lusard	Lusard	53	4.91	29.15
Publikum	public	100	9.26	28.93
Forfatteren	author (def.)	95	8.79	27.33
Claudine	Claudine	45	4.17	26.86
Nutiden	present day	45	4.17	26.21
Produktivitet	productivity, work	39	3.61	23.36
Andersens	Andersen's	32	2.96	22.65
Ferdinand	Ferdinand	30	2.78	21.53
Dalund	Dalund	28	2.59	21.19
Forfatterens	author's (def.,gen.)	30	2.78	20.11
Novellen	short story (def.)	28	2.59	19.65
Forfatter-Virksomhed	work as an author	29	2.68	19.08
Hr.	Mr.	60	5.55	18.97
Zerline	Zerline	30	2.78	18.62
Nivelleringen	levelling (def.)	21	1.94	18.35
Tidsalderens	ages' (def., gen.)	23	2.13	18.32
Forfatterskabet	authorship	20	1.85	17.91
Enten	either	46	4.26	17.60
Mariane	Mariane	23	2.13	17.54
Revolutions-Tiden	time of revolution	18	1.67	16.99
Hverdags-Historie	Story/Everyday Life	18	1.67	16.99
Enkelte	single individual	158	14.63	16.83
Madame	Madam	20	1.85	16.55
Dr.	Dr.	32	2.96	16.55
Nivelleringens	levelling (def.,gen.)	17	1.57	16.51
Principets	principle's (def.)	16	1.48	16.02
Noveller	short stories	23	2.13	15.91
religieus	religious	67	6.20	15.60
Waller	Waller	15	1.39	15.51
opbyggelige	edifying	41	3.80	15.23
Reflexionens	reflection's (def.)	34	3.15	15.12
Christian	Christian (name)	14	1.30	14.98
Beck	Beck	13	1.20	14.44
Corsaren	The Corsair	13	1.20	14.44
Bergland	Bergland	13	1.20	14.44
Deel	part	85	7.87	14.36
Efterskrift	Postscript	23	2.13	14.14
Literaturen	literature (def.)	18	1.67	14.08
Grosserer	wholesaler	13	1.20	13.85
Mængde	crowd	62	5.74	13.67
W.s	Waller's	11	1.02	13.28
Spillemand	fiddler, musician	11	1.02	13.28
Tidsalderen	age, period (def.)	12	1.11	13.26
Mazetto	Masetto	12	1.11	13.26
Udmærkede	honoured (subs.)	31	2.87	13.14
Reflexion	reflection	67	6.20	12.92
Categorie	category	25	2.31	12.84
Existeren	mode of existence	17	1.57	12.37
Decorum	decorum	12	1.11	12.22
lidenskabsløs	passionless	14	1.30	12.22
Mængden	crowd (def.)	46	4.26	12.15
Arnold	Arnold	9	0.83	12.01
Revolutionstiden	time of revolution	9	0.83	12.01
Troen	faith (def.)	4	0.37	-6.06
Kjerlighed	love	17	1.57	-7.49
Menneske	man	134	12.40	-9.57
Gud	God	116	10.74	-9.61
Du	you, Thou	94	8.70	-17.75

Table 6d. ABFREQ words in group 4 (T, TTL, . . . TAF, and GU)

Word	Trans./Use	Freq.	R.F.	S.D.
Kjerlighed	love	1404	24.94	44.79
Gud	God	2747	48.80	34.62
Du	Thou, You	4260	75.68	34.49
Kjerligheden	love (def.)	535	9.50	28.86
Fuglen	bird (def.)	519	9.22	27.81
Dig	Thou, You, Yourself	2288	40.65	26.89
Gode	(the) Good	745	13.23	24.80
Menneske	man	2514	44.66	24.09
elske	love (inf.)	639	11.35	21.45
Lilien	lily (def.)	293	5.21	21.30
Kjerlige	(the) lover	290	5.15	21.05
han	he	9133	162.25	21.00
den	it, he, she, that	14250	253.15	20.37
Næsten	neighbour (def.)	231	4.10	18.91
Talen	discourse (def.)	365	6.48	18.07
Bekymring	anxiety, worry	303	5.38	17.72
Thi	For (conj.)	672	11.94	17.36
Lidende	sufferer	274	4.87	17.24
Evighedens	eternity (def., gen.)	282	5.01	16.72
Kjerlighedens	love (def., gen.)	193	3.43	16.26
jo	yes, certainly	2377	42.23	16.02
Din	Thy, Thine	722	12.83	15.94
naar	if, when	2615	46.45	15.77
Guds	God's	530	9.42	15.52
Trængselen	crowd, throng (def.)	156	2.77	15.12
ham	him	3405	60.49	14.88
O	Oh	381	6.77	14.29
Forventning	expectation	185	3.29	14.16
Evigheden	eternity (def.)	372	6.61	14.11
ak	ah	279	4.96	14.04
Evige	Eternal (subs.)	364	6.47	13.98
Den	It, He, She, That	1851	32.88	13.64
Sjel	soul	311	5.52	13.49
Eet	one	344	6.11	13.33
m.T.	my hearer	117	2.08	13.22
Dit	Thy, Thine	407	7.23	13.20
Dag	day	444	7.89	13.14
Lydighed	obedience	139	2.47	13.10
dersom	if, in case	546	9.70	13.08
Taalmodigheden	patience (def.)	106	1.88	13.02
Ham	Him	215	3.82	13.00
Gave	gift	199	3.54	12.97
dog	however, still	3215	57.11	12.94
da	then, when, as	3848	68.36	12.68
Dødens	death's (def., gen.)	149	2.65	12.44
Bekymringen	anxiety (def.)	114	2.03	12.43
lære	teach	342	6.08	12.42
Ak	Ah	206	3.66	12.15
mon	I wonder (adv.)	147	2.61	11.90
Alteret	altar (def.)	100	1.78	11.85
Modgang	adversity	83	1.47	11.63
Tvesindethed	double-mindedness	79	1.40	11.59
vi	we	1331	23.64	11.57
Bekymrede	anxious (subs. pl.)	88	1.56	11.41
Trøst	consolation	214	3.80	11.31
Christendom	Christianity	36	0.64	-12.75
hendes	her, hers	85	1.51	-13.66
hun	she	396	7.03	-23.18
mig	me	600	10.66	-29.83
jeg	I (l.c.)	1387	24.64	-46.75

COMMENT ON McKINNON

Ralph H. Johnson

The results which Professor McKinnon has presented are enormous in scope, and it will take some time before they can be fully judged and appreciated. While the results strike me as being, on the whole, both accurate and interesting, I do have some reservations about some of them.

My first reservation concerns the similarity indices presented in tables 3b and 3c. For I do have a rather longstanding interest in AE and PS, and indeed in the relationship between these two works and their overall place in the authorship.

Now looking at table 3c, I find that the two works which McKinnon's study shows to be closest and most similar (at least in respect of ABFREQ vocabulary) to PS are, first, BA, and, second, AE. This result troubles me, if we are to take the ABFREQ similarity to be indicative of deeper conceptual and thematic similarity. For I would have thought that AE would have come out first. There are, to be sure, differences in style and vocabulary between the two works. Thus, terms like "subjectivity" and "inwardness," both of which play a central role in AE, make no appearance at all in PS. At the same time, terms like "the Teacher," "the disciple," and "the Moment in time," which are central to PS, make infrequent appearances in AE. And those differences are perhaps just what McKinnon's computer has caught.

However, let us be somewhat circumspect here, remembering that our pseudonymous author, Johannes Climacus, prides himself on being able to say essentially the same thing in different ways.

I must admit, then, that the placing of BA ahead of AE is a result which is not in general accord with my own preconceptions. Briefly, my reasons are these. First, both PS and AE are committed to the Socratic view that subjectivity, inwardness is the truth. The vocabulary they use to make this point is different, but the thesis is the same in both works. Moreover, I would argue that this thesis is central and characteristic of these two works in a fashion that is not clearly true in the case of BA. Second, here is what Climacus has to say about BA: "The Concept of Dread differs essentially from the other pseudonymous writings in having a direct form, and in being even a little bit objectively dogmatic."[12] On the other hand, both PS and AE are indirect, or so I would be prepared to argue, and could not by any stretch of the imagination be termed "a little bit objectively dogmatic."

Exactly the same misgivings crop up when we look at table 3c for AE's relatives, which turn out to be, first, BA, and, second, SV. And where, pray tell, is PS, to which this work, after all, is a postscript? Well, according to table 3b, and by my reckoning, PS is no closer than ninth, coming in behind the two already cited works and also BI, EE1, EE2, IC, KG, and Ø. But can this really be right? Can all these works be more similar, in fundamental respects, to PS, than is AE?

I find this result difficult to assimilate, as does another well-known commentator who has stated: "The argument of the Fragments is formal and at times algebraic while its mood is often somber and, on occasion, not unlike that of The Concept of Dread. Postscript, on the other hand, is gay and even hilarious and has an inner momentum much like that of certain parts of Either/Or."[13] Now the commentator who wrote this would certainly balk, I would think, at placing BA as AE's closest relative in the corpus. Now we might simply ascribe this difference of opinion to the well-known variances within Kierkegaard research . . . except for the fact that the commentator whose opinion I have just quoted is none other than Professor McKinnon himself in an earlier article! What we have here is an apparent conflict between the earlier McKinnon and the later, and I am most curious to find out what the current McKinnon will have to say.

While I find the similarity indices disconcerting for the

works mentioned above, I should mention, on the other side of the ledger, that the results seem right on target in other instances. For example, SV turns out to have EE1 and EE2 as its closest relatives, which certainly accords with my own instincts.

Let me bring my remarks about the similarity indices to a close by stating that I have to express reservations about the assumption behind them, which McKinnon puts this way: "the number or, better, the percentage of such aberrant frequency words which two works have in common is a very accurate and percipient measure of their similarity."[14] I have indicated some reasons for my misgivings about this assumption. Let me suggest where the fly in the ointment is. The computer lacks inwardness! Detecting and appreciating the deeper conceptual and thematic similarities in this complex authorship requires inwardness. Until Professor McKinnon can program inwardness into the computer——a task which I believe lies beyond even his considerable talent and imagination——I think these deeper similarities must escape.

I wanted to comment on the clusters which McKinnon's study has produced. For they strike me, on the whole, as accurate. But I think I have said quite enough as it is. I only hope that these comments and questions, and those that are sure to come from others here present, will help to clarify further both the nature and the value of the work that McKinnon has shared with us today, and will help to chart the course of its future development.

NOTES

Notes to Chapter 4 (Cappelørn/Retrospective Understanding)

1. I should like to take this opportunity to express my thanks to Michael Plekon for assistance in translating this paper into English.
2. Pap. X 1 A 421.
3. SV XIII, 534; cf. FV, 154.
4. Pap. X 3 B 4.
5. Pap. X 2 A 158; cf. JP 6, 6522.
6. Pap. X 2 A 242; cf. JP 6, 6547.
7. SV XIII, 74.
8. Pap. IV A 164; cf. JP 1, 1030.
9. SV XIII, 529; cf. FV, 147.
10. Pap. X 6 B 146, p. 220.
11. Walter Lowrie, Kierkegaard (Princeton: Princeton University Press, 1946), 107.
12. Pap. IV C 37; cf. JP 3, 2367.
13. Pap. V A 74; cf. JP 3, 2341.
14. Pap. V C 12; cf. JP 3, 2352.
15. Pap. V B 1, 3; cf. JP 3, 2342.
16. Pap. II A 118; cf. JP 5, 5241.
17. Pap. X 5 A 146; cf. JP 6, 6843.
18. Pap. VIII 1 A 424; cf. JP 5, 6078.
19. See Henning Fenger, Kierkegaard-Myter og Kierkegaard-Kilder (Odense: Odense Universitetsforlag, 1976), 35-56.

20. Pap. VII 1 A 222; cf. JP 5, 5962.

21. Pap. X 1 A 442.

22. Pap. X 5 A 105; cf. JP 6, 6840.

23. Pap. X 1 A 239; cf. JP 6, 6380.

24. SV XIII, 551; cf. SFV, 5.

25. The original is quoted in SV XIII, 548 and the translation in SFV, 2.

26. SV XII, 17; cf. IC, 7.

27. Pap. X 6 B 196, p. 308.

28. SV XIII, 528; cf. FV, 146.

29. SV XIII, 558; cf. SFV, 13.

30. SV XIII, 531; cf. FV, 150.

31. Ibid.

32. SV XIII, 557; cf. SFV, 13.

33. SV XIII, 556; cf. SFV, 10f.

34. SV XIII, 556; cf. SFV, 12.

35. Pap. X 3 A 143; cf. JP 3, 3357.

36. SV III, 15; cf. T, 21.

37. SV XIII, 553; cf. SFV, 8.

38. SV XIII, 529; cf. FV, 148.

39. Pap. X 2 A 642, p. 464; cf. JP 4, 4460.

40. Ibid.

41. SV VII, 98; cf. AE, 108.

Notes to Chapter 5 (Hong/Tanke-Experiment)

1. JP 6, 6407; cf. Pap. X 1 A 351.

2. SV I, 4.

3. Emanuel Hirsch, Kierkegaard-Studien, I $^{1-2}$-III $^{1-3}$ (Gütersloh: Bertelsman Verlag, 1933), III ^{2}, 95.

4. Pap. IV B 1, pp. 146-50.

5. Johannes Climacus, or De omnibus dubitandum est, trans. by T. H. Croxall (London: Black, 1958), 66, 88, 148, 150.

6. SV VIII, 96; cf. LA, 103 and also the relevant notes and entries in Supplement.

7. Pap. VII 1 B 110, p. 318. See also Pap. VIII 2 B 81:10, p. 147; X 4 A 614, p. 430.

8. Second and third editions (Copenhagen: 1844, 1853; ASKB 1034-35).

9. JP 5, 5657; cf. Pap. IV B 97:1.

10. This is also the case in German. Grimms Wörterbuch does not have Experiment as a rubric, only Erfahrung and Versuch, etc. Kierkegaard had Anton T. Brück's German translation of Bacon's Novum Organum (Leipzig: 1830; ASKB 420). In the English version "experiment" etc. are used hundreds of times; in the Latin various forms of experientia are used. The German translation very rarely has Experiment but rather uses Versuch, Untersuchung, Empiriker (for "men of experiment"), etc. In Hegel, according to Hermann Glockner, Hegel-Lexicon I-II (Stuttgart: Fromanns Verlag, 1957), I, 581, the term Experiment is used only once, in Wissenschaft der Logik, Werke V, 299 (J. A. V, 299); Hegel's Science of Logic, trans. by A. V. Miller (London: Allen & Unwin, 1969; New York: Humanities Press, 1969), 802. Experiment there refers to the presentation to intuition of a particular case of the specific character apprehended by cognition.

11. See Index Verborum til Kierkegaards Samlede Værker, comp. by Alastair McKinnon (Leiden: E. J. Brill, 1973 and Princeton: Princeton University Press, 1979); and indexes to Søren Kierkegaards Papirer XIV-XVI, comp. by N. J. Cappelørn (Copenhagen: Gyldendal, 1975-78).

12. "The Activity of a Traveling Esthetician," Ordbog over det Danske Sprog I-XXVIII (Copenhagen: 1919-56), quotes the expression with a symbolic comet, meaning "extremely rare, unique."

13. Pap. II C 4 in suppl. vol. XIII, p. 151. The Danish gjøre Erfaringer is translated literally. See JP 2, 2251 (Pap. IV C 46, 1837) and note 721.

14. JP 1, 136 (Pap. II A 352, 5 February 1839).

15. JP 5, 5608 (Pap. IV C 127, 1842-43).

16. JP 1, 144 (Pap. IV C 109, 1842-43). See SV, 395 (SV VI, 407).

17. JP 5, 5592 (Pap. IV C 24, 1842-43).

18. Preparation for receptivity to this view of poetry and its substance was most likely provided by Kierkegaard's earlier reading of Plato, particularly the Phaedo, in which Socrates says (61 b) that "a poet, if he is worthy of the name, ought to work on imaginative themes, not on descriptive ones . . . ." The substance of the dialogue is drawn upon twice (60 b, 97-99) in Either/Or (finished in November 1842 and published 20 February 1843), SV I, 208, 209.

19. G. E. Lessings sämmtliche Schriften I-XXXII (Berlin: 1825-28; ASKB 1747-62). Lessing's view is epitomized on p. 249: "In a fable, the fable-maker only wants to bring an idea into perceptible form [Intuition]."

20. JP 3, 2373 (Pap. X 1 A 363, 1849).

21. Pap. VI 98:21.

22. SV VII, 48.

23. See, for example, JP 1, 1059; 6, 6440, 6870 (Pap. X 2 A 439; X 1 A 531; XI 1 A 131).

24. JP 1, 1059 (Pap. X 2 A 439).

25. PS, 95 (SV IV, 242).

26. JP 1, 1058 (Pap. X 2 A 414). Cf. the first page of Frater Taciturnus's "Letter to the Reader," SV, 363 (SV VI, 371).

27. Pap. IV B 79, 1843.

28. Åge Henriksen, Kierkegaards Romaner (Copenhagen: Gyldendal, 1969), 8-9.

29. JP 5, 5865 (Pap. VII 1 A 83) states that "'Guilty?'/'Not Guilty?'" in Stages is the imaginary construction par excellence in that it not only is in the form of double reflection, as all the pseudonymous works are, but that the Quidam of the imaginary construction also makes an imaginary construction in order "to poetize himself out of a girl." On the other hand, the second imaginary construction in the Quidam sense is "lacking in Either/Or" (JP 5, 5866; Pap. VII 1 A 84, 1846), an omission that is explained in JP 5, 5628 (Pap. IV A 215, 1843): "The only thing this work lacks is a narrative, which I did begin but omitted, just as Aladdin left a window incomplete. It was to be called 'Unhappy Love.' It was to form a contrast to the Seducer."

30. JP 1, 3846 (Pap. I C 69, October 1835).

31. JP 1, 633 (Pap. VI 13 40:45, 1845).

32. Francis Bacon, Novum Organum I, xcviii. See note 10.

33. Gæa (1846), 176-78.

34. Georg Brandes (ed. and trans.), Søren Kierkegaard, Samlede Skrifter I-XVIII (Copenhagen: 1899-1910), II, 292.

35. The text of the manuscript is printed in Hjalmar Helweg (ed. and trans.), Søren Kierkegaard (Copenhagen: 1933), 385-92. The quoted portion is from p. 386

36. SV I, 10.

37. Cited in Richard E. Palmer, Hermeneutics (Evanston: Northwestern University Press, 1969), 27-8.

Notes to Chapter 6 (Walker/Communication)

1. KG, 351.
2. KG, 211.
3. CT, 120-23.
4. KG, 225.
5. KG, 260.
6. KG, 336.
7. KG, 351f.
8. See, KG 257.
9. JP 2, 1957; cf. Pap. IX A 221.
10. SFV, 115.
11. KG, 225.

Notes to Chapter 7 (Carignan/The Eternal)

1. Kierkegaard had just written Judge For Yourselves which he considered too virulent for publication at that time. In it he launched a strong attack on the official Danish church and its highest-ranking prelate, Bishop Mynster.
2. JP 1, 80 (Pap. X 4 A 638).
3. Ibid.
4. JP 4, 4483 (Pap. XI 1 A 475).
5. Pap. VIII 1 A 312; X 4 A 482; XI 1 A 408, 592; XI 2 A 246.
6. The Concept of Dread, trans. by Walter Lowrie (Princeton: Princeton University Press, 1957), 76.
7. The Sickness Unto Death, trans. by Walter Lowrie (Princeton: Princeton University Press, 1941), 17.
8. See Mark C. Taylor, Kierkegaard's Pseudonymous Authorship (Princeton: Princeton University Press, 1975), 94-108.
9. In fact, Anti-Climacus says "Faith is: that the self in being itself and in willing to be itself is grounded transparently in God." Sickness, 132.
10. Among the most recent in French and English are: André Clair, "L'homme malade et la santé comme tâche," Rev. Sc. Phil. Théol. 54 (1970), 489-515 and 619-635; Pseudonymie et Paradoxe (Paris: Vrin, 1967); Mark C. Taylor, "Kierkegaard on the Structure of Selfhood," Kierkegaardiana 9 (1974), 84-101;

Mark C. Taylor, Authorship, 81-126; and John W. Elrod, Being and Existence in Kierkegaard's Works (Princeton: Princeton University Press, 1975). Mention should also be made of the less recent articles by Robert S. Hartman, "The Self in Kierkegaard," Journal of Existential Psychiatry 2 (1962), 409-436; Louis Dupré, "The Constitution of the Self in Kierkegaard's Philosophy," International Philosophical Quarterly 3 (1963), 506-526; Paul Dietrichson, "Kierkegaard's Concept of the Self," Inquiry 8 (1965), 1-32; and Jacques Colette, "Le désir d'être soi et la fonction du Père chez Kierkegaard," L'Inconscient 5 (Jan.-Mar. 1968), 131-155.

11. Chap. 3, 81-126.

12. Dread, 79.

13. Sickness, 43.

14. Dread, 81. (Our underlining to stress the difficulty of interpretation.)

15. Ibid., 76.

16. Either/Or 2 trans. by Walter Lowrie (Princeton: Princeton University Press, 1949) 180.

17. Sickness, 43.

18. Either/Or 2, 147.

19. JP 2, 1249 (Pap. V B 56:2).

20. Dread, 96.

21. Ibid., 97.

22. Ibid., 38.

23. Ibid., 45.

24. Ibid., 45.

25. Ibid., 45.

26. JP 2, 1261 (Pap. X 2 A 428).

27. Ibid.

28. Ibid.

29. JP 2, 1268 (Pap. X 4 A 175).

30. Ibid.

31. Ibid.

32. Pap. IV B 111.

33. JP 2, 1269 (Pap. X 4 A 177).

34. JP 3, 2365; 3, 2366; 2, 1241 (Pap. IV C 31, 36, 39).

35. Dread, 45.

36. As is demonstrated in convincing fashion by Nelly Viallaneix in an article, Kierkegaard had great admiration for Leibniz, quoting him profusely in the Journals from November 1842 to March 1844, even singing his praises, something he was not wont to do for a philosopher: "Kierkegaard, lecteur de Leibniz," in Critique (Revue générale des publications françaises et étrangères), October 1969, 895-914.

37. Leibniz wrote: "All is therefore certain and determined beforehand in man, as everywhere else, and the human soul is a kind of spiritual automaton, although contingent actions in general and free action in particular are not on that account necessary with an absolute necessity, which would be truly incompatible with contingency." Theodicy, Part 1, Section 52. His entire position on freedom is clearly set forth in Fragment H: "Libertas indifferentiae est impossibilis. Adeo ut ne in Deum quidem cadat, nam determinatus ille est ad optimum efficiendum. Et creaturae semper ex rationibus internis externisque determinantur. Quo plus substantiae sunt per se determinatae et ab indifferentia remotae, eo sunt perfectiones . . . . Eo major est libertas, quo magis agitur ex ratione, et eo major est servitus, quo magis agitur ex animi passionibus." C. I. Gerhardt, Die philosophischen Schriften von G. W. Leibniz, 8, 109.

38. JP 2, 1269 (Pap. X 4 A 177). (Our underlining).

39. Sickness, 17.

40. Taylor, Authorship, 117.

41. See "An ecstatic lecture" in Either/Or 1, 37-42 (SV I, 26-31). The alternative confronting the estheticist is a true dilemma. Whether one chooses this or that, one will in any event regret one's choice. Therefore Estheticist A's option is to withdraw into the eternity of the imagination which, through indifference, reconciles the elements of the dilemma. But this is basically a useless masquerade to permit the estheticist to try to camouflage indefinitely his non-commitment. Judge William denounces the vanity and frivolity of his friend A: "Do you not know that there comes a midnight when everyone has to throw off his mask? Do you believe that life will always let itself be mocked? Do you think you can slip away a little before midnight in order to avoid this?" Either/Or 2, 135.

42. Taylor, Authorship, 117.

43. JP 4, 4339. (Pap. X 3 A 705).

44. Ibid., 4361. (Pap. XI 2 A 317).

45. Ibid., 4362. (Pap. XI 2 A 353).

46. Ibid., 4363. (Pap. XI 2 A 378). See also Pour un examen de conscience, Oeuvres Complètes (Gallimard) 18, 77ff.; and L'Instant.

47. "On My Work as an Author," SFV, 142-164 (SV XIII, 522-543); see also Cornelio Fabro, "La Missione di Kierkegaard," in Ethica 8 (1969), 169-80.

48. Sickness, 67.

49. Here we draw on Paul Dietrichson's penetrating analysis, "Kierkegaard's

Concept of the Self," in Inquiry 8 (1965), 1-32.

50. Either/Or 2, 181.

51. Ibid., 148.

52. Ibid., 152.

53. Pap. X 4 A 177.

54. AE, 85.

55. Either/Or 2, 190.

56. Ibid., 190-1.

57. Ibid., 174.

58. Carignan, 83.

59. The Journals of Kierkegaard, ed. and trans. by Alexander Dru (London: Fontana Books, 1967), 181-82. Cf. Pap. X 2 A 396

60. Carignan, 83.

61. Ibid.

62. Ibid., 85.

63. Ibid., 81.

64. Ibid., 79.

65. Ibid., 81-2.

66. Ibid., 81, 87.

Notes to Chapter 8 (Nielsen/Indirect Communication)

1. G. Bornkamm, Jesus of Nazareth, trans. by I. and F. McLuskey (New York: Harper and Row, 1960). Speaking of gospel miracle stories Bornkamm remarks that "precisely in this area of the tradition many stories have taken on legendary traits, and legends have been added. This applies particularly, though not exclusively, to the 'nature miracles' in the narrower sense of the term" (131). Among these Bornkamm includes the walking on the waves (note 40, 208). In R. H. Fuller's Interpreting the Miracles (London: S.C.M. Press, 1963), which expressly designates Mark 6:45-52 as a construction by the early church (59), we find this general statement: "Coming to the New Testament miracles, modern man is prepared to accept the healings of Jesus as due to his power of suggestion: the nature miracles . . . he can only dismiss as pious legend" (121). On the following page Fuller aligns himself with "the modern critical believer" over against "the fundamentalist" in a division which, this reader hopes, is not intended to exhaust all possible positions. In a passage about the nature miracles in B. Vawter's This Man Jesus: An Essay Toward a New Testament Christology (Garden City, N. Y.:

Doubleday, 1973) we find this: "The legend is not, usually, without all foundation, and often it is a sure index of character, since legends, as we have continually pointed out, do not collect about a colorless individual; but for all that, it is legend and must be read as such" (143). The passage opens with this surprising sentence: "To begin with, the so-called nature miracles do not, generally speaking, have the immediate connection with the gospel kerygma that is proper to the miracles of healing" (121-22).

2. AE, 518.

3. Mark 6, not without some initiative from the reader, reveals an unthinkable state indirectly. This does not mean that thinking about that state is forever at a standstill, or that the concomitants of that state cannot be thought. For example a person can examine the choices he has made and the judgments, formed or otherwise, which those choices indirectly disclose. I have looked into this in some detail in "The Concept of Sin Consciousness" in New Themes in Christian Philosophy, ed. R. McInerny (Notre Dame: University of Notre Dame Press, 1968).

Notes to Chapter 9 (Khan/Lidenskab in Efterskrift)

1. See Alastair McKinnon, "From Co-occurrences to Concepts," Computers and the Humanities 11 (May/June 1977), 147-55. Equally helpful in following this method are two of his other articles "Similarities and Differences in Kierkegaard's Accounts of Hegel," Kierkegaardiana 10 (Copenhagen, 1977), 119-32 and "A Method of Displaying Differences Between Various Accounts of an Object," revue CIRPHO review 2, 1 (Spring 1974), 31-57.

2. The importance of this concept is obvious from a line appearing almost at the very end of Efterskrift. It reads: " . . . selv Den, der fortabes i Lidenskab, har ikke tabt saa meget som Den der tabte Lidenskab." (" . . . he who loses himself through passion has not lost as much as he who has lost passion.") SV 10, 273; cf. AE, 540.

3. See note 1.

4. James Deese has advanced this postulate in the report of his studies on the structure of association in the English language. It is interesting to note that this study appears to suggest that the same principle of association seems to hold also in the Danish language. See James Deese, The Structure of Association in Language and Thought (Baltimore: Johns Hopkins University Press, 1965).

5. SV 10, 51; cf. AE, 313.

6. Ibid., 9, 31; cf. AE, 33 (my translation).

7. Ibid., 9, 147; cf. AE, 157.

8. Ibid., 9, 31, 32; cf. AE, 32, 33.

9. Ibid., 10, 241; cf. AE, 509.

10. Ibid., 9, 27, 32; cf. AE, 28, 33.

11. Ibid., 9, 50, 51; cf. AE, 53, 54.

12. Ibid., 9, 32; cf. AE, 33.

13. Ibid., 10, 186; cf. AE, 456.

14. Ibid., 10, 81; cf. AE, 345.

15. Ibid., 9, 169-71; cf. AE, 181-83.

16. Ibid., 9, 166, 171; cf. AE, 177, 183.

17. Ibid., 9, 192; cf. AE, 206.

18. Ibid., 9, 175, 194; cf. AE, 188, 209.

19. Ibid., 9, 27; cf. AE, 28.

20. To paraphrase Wittgenstein, we are unable to notice certain features because they are always before our eyes. Compare Wittgenstein's remark, "(Man kann es nicht bemerken,——weil man es immer vor Augen hat.)" Philosophical Investigations (Oxford: Blackwell, 1967) prop. 129, with that of Rousseau's "Il faut beaucoup de philosophie pour savoir observer une fois ce qu'on voit tous les jours." The comparison and quotation from Rousseau are cited in John Passmore, Philosophical Reasoning, (New York: Charles Scribner's Sons, 1961) 10.

Notes to Chapter 10 (McKinnon/Shape of Authorship)

1. Alastair McKinnon, "Aberrant Frequencies as a Basis for Clustering the Works of a Corpus," revue CIRPHO review 3, 1 (Spring 1975-76), 33-52.

2. KYST is the acronymic title for the Kruskal-Young-Shephard-Torgerson Multidimensional Scaling program written by Dr. J. B. Kruskal, Bell Telephone Laboratories, Murray Hill, N.J. and Dr. F. W. Young, Psychometric Laboratory, University of North Carolina, Chapel Hill, N.C., assisted by Judith Seery, Bell Telephone Laboratories, Murray Hill, N.J.

3. Alastair McKinnon, "Aberrant Frequency Words: Their Identification and Uses," Glottometrika 2 (Bochum: Studienverlag Brockmeyer, 1980), 108-24.

4. Joseph B. Kruskal and Myron Wish, Multidimensional Scaling (Beverly Hills and London: Sage Publications, 1978), 30-35.

5. SFV, 10-22; cf. SV 18, 85-92.

6. AE, 261; cf. also SFV, 10-14, JP 4, 4454 (Pap. X 1 A 134) and JP 4, 4472 (Pap. X 4 A 251), etc.

7. Søren Kierkegaard, On Authority and Revelation, ed. and trans. by Walter Lowrie (New York: Harper Torchbooks, 1966), lvii.

8. Ibid., lvii.

9. Ibid., Preface No. 3, lv-lxiii.

10. Ibid., lvii.

11. Pap. X 6 B 144, pp. 197-244.

12. AE, 241.

13. Alastair McKinnon, "Kierkegaard's Pseudonyms: A New Hierarchy", American Philosophical Quarterly, 6, 123.

14. McKinnon, 124.

CONTRIBUTORS

R. H. ARCHER is Associate Professor of Philosophy and Classics at the University of Regina and is concerned with the application of existentialist insights to certain current social issues.

Niels Jørgen CAPPELØRN is the General Secretary of the Danish Bible Society. He has published Søren Kierkegaards Papirer, Vol. XIV-XVI, Index A-Ø og Bibelindex, Copenhagen, 1975-78 as well as articles on Kierkegaard, including two with Alastair McKinnon.

Maurice CARIGNAN is Associate Professor in the Department of Philosophy at the University of Ottawa. He is the author of Individu et Société chez Kierkegaard (Halifax, 1977) and a number of articles on Kierkegaard. At present he is working on Philosophical Fragments and Edifying Discourses.

Peter A. CARPENTER has been teaching recently in the Faculty of Religious Studies of McGill University. He has published articles on and a translation of Thévenaz and has an article forthcoming on Sartre.

David GOICOECHEA is Associate Professor of Philosophy at Brock University. He has published articles on Kierkegaard and Royce and at the moment is working on Being in Love, a study of the historical and phenomenological relation of these two concepts.

Howard V. HONG is Professor Emeritus of St. Olaf College and the Director of the Kierkegaard Library. With Edna H. Hong he is the editor and translator of Søren Kierkegaards Journals and Papers, 1 - 7 (Indiana, 1967-78) and General Editor of Kierkegaard's Writings (Princeton, 1978-). At last word he and his wife were editing and translating The Concept of Irony and Either/Or.

Ralph H. JOHNSON is Professor of Philosophy at the University of Windsor and has published The Concept of Existence in the Concluding Unscientific Postscript and "Kierkegaard on Philosophy." He is presently working on informal logic and Kierkegaard's theory of the stages.

Abrahim H. KHAN has held appointments at the University of Manitoba, the University of Toronto and McGill University. He has published papers on Kierkegaard, Islam and Hinduism and is currently working mainly on Kierkegaard, Wittgenstein and Tagore.

David LOCHHEAD is Associate Professor in the Department of History and Theology of the Vancouver School of Theology. His publications include The Liberation of the Bible, The Lordship of Jesus and Living Between Memory and Hope. His current work is in the field of hermeneutics.

Alastair McKINNON is Macdonald Professor of Moral Philosophy and Chairman of the Department of Philosophy at McGill University. He has published Falsification and Belief (The Hague, 1970 and California, 1978) and many papers including some on Kierkegaard and some on the use of the computer in the interpretation of texts. He has compiled The Kierkegaard Indices, (Leiden, 1970-75 and Princeton, 1979) and is currently engaged, with Hans Kaal, in similar work on Wittgenstein.

Joseph C. McLELLAND is McConnell Professor of Philosophy of Religion and Dean of The Faculty of Religious Studies of McGill University. He has published _The Visible Words of God_ (Edinburgh, 1957), _God the Anonymous_ (Philadelphia, 1976) and edited _Peter Martyr Vermigli and Italian Reform_ (Waterloo, 1980). His current research concerns "the irony of atheism" and is an examination of the Prometheus myth since the Enlightenment.

Hans MÖLLER is now Director of the Graduate School of Library Science at McGill University. He has published _Media for Discovery_ (Toronto, 1970) and various articles and book reviews in professional journals in the field of library science.

Harry A. NIELSEN is Professor of Philosophy at the University of Windsor. He has published four books and thirty articles and is now mainly concerned with Darwinian myths about man and with contemporary moral issues.

Robert L. PERKINS is Professor of Philosophy at the University of South Alabama. He has published a number of articles on Hegel and Kierkegaard, including some on the latter's social thought. He has recently edited _Kierkegaard's "Fear and Trembling": Critical Appraisals_ (Alabama, 1981).

H. P. ROHDE is a distinguished Danish historian of art and culture who has written many books including _The Auctioneer's Sales Record of the Library of S. Kierkegaard_ (Copenhagen, 1967) and _Enigmatical Stages on the Way of S. Kierkegaard_ (Copenhagen, 1974). His major work on a painting of Constantin Hansen is to be published in 1982.

Jeremy WALKER is Associate Professor of Philosophy at McGill University. He has done extensive work on Kierkegaard on whom he has published several papers as well as _To Will One Thing_ (Montreal, 1972). He has also published a book on Frege.